NORTH YORK PUBLIC LIBRARY
CDA

D1450310

WITHDRAWN
From Toronto Public Library

Daisy

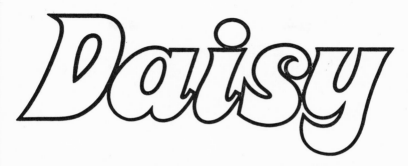

**THE FASCINATING STORY OF DAISY SMITH,
WIFE OF DR. OSWALD J. SMITH,
MISSIONARY STATESMAN AND FOUNDER
OF THE PEOPLES CHURCH, TORONTO**

Hope Evangeline

Baker Book House
Grand Rapids, Michigan

Copyright 1978 by
Baker Book House Company

ISBN: 0-8010-3328-4

*Printed in the United States
of America*

All Scripture quotations are taken
from the King James Version of the Bible
unless otherwise stated.

TO

Daisy's Nine Grandchildren

Peter, Pauline and Paul

June, Bruce and Christopher

Glen, Jann and Jill

NORTH YORK PUBLIC LIBRARY
CDA

ACKNOWLEDGMENTS

*Thanks to Norma Cooper
for her encouragement and help
in collecting the material for this book
Thanks to my son Paul James
for his many suggestions and help
in editing*

AUTHOR'S NOTE

*Throughout this biographical novel
I have tried to follow closely the details
and events of Daisy's long life, changing only
for dramatic reasons or for lack of more accurate
information. I have used real names except
for a few characters whose names I
was unable to obtain.*

Contents

Preface

What nearer, sweeter union could there be?
Wife, husband, home, and love, the best of all,
All knit in one, a bond with none more dear
By God ordained long years before the fall. *

These words were written in 1918. Perhaps the chaos and upheaval of those turbulent times motivated the author. When the whole social fabric is shaken to its very roots, men invariably are drawn closer to hearth and home, wherein lies some vestige of security and meaning in life. The strain of war has frequently challenged all forms of human organization. And almost as frequently the existing social order has failed to meet the challenges successfully and crumbled. Men lose faith in governments, in institutions, in religious systems and in human wisdom. In that hour of global desperation we turn so often to the most basic unit of life—the family. The ancient trinity, a man and woman united before God, has sustained the race through perpetual conflict and turmoil for as long as history records.

It is not surprising that in that year a young Canadian preacher, Oswald Smith, should pen the verse we have quoted. He had been married twenty months. His first son was not yet

*From the poem entitled "Wife" in Oswald J. Smith, *Poems of a Lifetime* (London: Marshall, Morgan and Scott, 1962), p. 50.

one year old. The world had been brutally ripped asunder in the greatest war yet seen. Apocalypse was in the air. Yet in these few lines there is a serenity, a strength, a peace that seems to defy reason. One can almost reach out and touch it. You can see it in the sense that you see a rugged pine or stately mountain.

The woman of whom Oswald wrote was his wife Daisy. She was everything her name implies. Rugged, she flourished anywhere against incredible hardship. Yet the beauty of her God was reflected daily in her countenance and in her life. She would sway and sometimes bend, but never break. This is her story.

These are days of extensive social upheaval, not unlike those of 1918. Once again the sword of Damocles hangs precariously over our civilization. International chaos is more prevalent than ever and humanity is under a sure threat of extinction from a multiplicity of dangers. Moreover, the winds of change also howl through the cracking plaster of our homes. The foundations are shifting, sinking. The embers on the hearth are cold, the pages of the family Bible are dusty, and the candles on the family altar are burned out.

Everyone is searching interminably for freedom. This search has taken women from their homes. Perhaps they will yet learn that the only freedom they can ever hope to own is freedom to choose with what chains they will be bound. Today's freedom is just another word for nothing left to lose.

In reviewing Daisy's life, I am convinced that we will all pay dearly for our new freedoms. The turmoil, conflict, strain and misery will still be there; the family under God will not. Where then will we turn to find the rock upon which to rebuild a ravished world? This is the story of a liberated woman. Early in her life she experienced the power that can free men and women, black and white, Gentile and Jew. She freely chose to be bound by chains of love for her husband and her God.

Paul James Lowry
grandson of Daisy Smith
and younger son of the author
(Vancouver, 1976)

Foreword

The once sturdy stem of the little flower, "Our Daisy," was soon to be broken, and we knew no man could mend it. She was eighty-two years of age, and for almost a year the petals were falling off one by one from this fragile blossom.

As I watched her life ebbing away inch by inch, like the various shades of a beautiful sunset slowly fading, I thought— God did not create this life and for eighty-two years seek to bring it to perfection, only to have it snuffed out by death! The musician does not struggle over his compositions, just to have them buried and forgotten when he dies. The artist does not labor for years to create a beautiful painting, pouring his very soul into it, just to have someone come along and destroy it.

Of course not! God had a purpose in all He had put into her, and in all He had brought her through. He was not only preparing Daisy for a greater life to come, but I feel sure He wanted others to be inspired and to take courage from a life spent for that which would outlast her living.

Memory is such a wonderful thing. Nothing can build a hedge around it. The door always swings open on its hinges. We can go in and out whenever we please. During the last few months of Daisy's life she was able to take many trips into the past and as she enjoyed it all over again, she shared it with her family.

She often recalled the roughness of the road, as she wandered through the valleys, and climbed the hard steep slopes of the mountain side. There were slippery rocks and wild branches moistened with tears, but she could always look up and see heaven's rainbow shining through.

As she wound her way in and out of the past in those precious last months with us, she enjoyed again the many glorious experiences on the mountain top as well, the showers of blessings and joys that were hers.

I could hardly bear to think of the day when the last petal would fall from this fragrant life. What could I do? Was there not some way I could preserve it?

When I expressed my desire to record the story, she seemed to live again on the inside, though she was withering and fading slowly away on the outside. Day after day during the remaining months of her life, she spent countless hours, with what little strength she had left, relating the past for the benefit of others.

I began filling page after page of the book I had visualized as she told me the fascinating story in her own inimitable way.

After you have read her story you will realize that she, unlike many women of today, knew the meaning of freedom.

Hope Evangeline

Part One

1

Early Childhood

It had been one of those steaming midsummer days typical of southern Ontario in July. Twilight brought relief from the infernal, hazy atmosphere blanketing Peterborough and the sultry farmlands cradling it. The crickets had already struck up their endless repetitive chorus, soon to be joined by the whippoorwill and a host of other familiar night sounds. The summer of 1885 had been one of the hottest and dryest in recent memory and James McIntyre had thought that perhaps the thunderheads which had glowered over the thirsty fields all afternoon would finally burst, pouring life-giving water upon the parched crops.

As he closed the barn door latch and turned toward the house, James glanced once more at the darkening sky, this time less hopeful as he noticed most of the storm clouds inoffensively dissipating in the east.

"Ready for supper, Father?" Minnie tossed the words over her shoulder as the screen door clapped shut behind her father. Minnie, the eldest of his four children, was sixteen and fast becoming an adult, as James was so painfully aware. For an instant she reminded him of his wife,

Elizabeth, in the early months and years of their marriage. Her brown eyes dancing and golden curls tied neatly back, she went cheerfully about her seemingly endless domestic chores, cooking this, cleaning that, mending and helping.

Minnie had the same self-confidence that her mother had. Everything she did seemed carefully considered. She had the same quiet assurance that having assessed a situation prudently, she need not fear the outcome of any particular action. James called it "judgment." "You have good judgment, Elizabeth," he was often heard to say, a compliment which his wife always accepted humbly and in silence.

James was brought quickly back from his reverie as Minnie, turning now to face him squarely with her hands on her hips, repeated, "Father, are you ready for supper?"

"Sure, Minnie. Isn't Mama home yet? Perhaps we should wait."

"Now, Father, you know it's a long way to Hastings and Mama loves to visit with cousin Alice. She so seldom gets the chance to be off on her own. She may be very late. The others are hungry and I've got things all ready."

Minnie's logic was, as usual, more than James was prepared to challenge. He disappeared upstairs to gather the rest of the family. As Minnie turned back to the stove, she heard a buggy rumble into the yard and her mother's friendly voice exchanging parting words with neighbors. The buggy rattled off and moments later her mother stood inside the kitchen.

"Well, Minnie, I see you're just one step ahead of me!" she exclaimed without noticing the table spread with the evening meal. Minnie had no chance to answer. Suddenly the kitchen swarmed with the younger children scrambling for their places at the table, closely followed by their father. Then, she and Minnie joined the others at the table and everyone bowed their heads as James gave thanks.

"You sure taught Minnie a thing or two about cooking, Elizabeth," James exclaimed.

"It's a good thing I have," replied Elizabeth, casting a searching glance at Minnie.

James asked all about the trip to Hastings—how was so-and-so, did cousin Alice still want to move to Peterborough, and a host of other questions. Elizabeth seemed preoccupied as she replied, so James fell silent.

Suddenly, Elizabeth dropped her fork and looking directly at Minnie, asked, "James, do you know that boy George Billings in town?" Minnie was paralyzed. Her eyes stared in vacant disbelief.

Elizabeth seemed to draw courage from James's qualified approval and continued, still scanning Minnie's terror-stricken eyes. "Well, when I was in Hastings today, I was told that our daughter, Minnie, actually married George Billings about two weeks ago." The table was instantly silent. Minnie clutched her fork even tighter, her knuckles ashen white and the color drained from her pretty face.

The stillness seemed endless. Minnie searched her father's face for an indication of his reaction to her mother's sudden announcement. His face was stern, but not angry, more contemplative than shocked. Then, glancing again at her mother she thought she detected a faint smile. Finally James spoke. "If this is true, Minnie—" he paused, perhaps hoping for a vehement denial of his wife's revelation as scurrilous rumor, a denial he would surely have welcomed and easily believed. He started again, "If this is true, Minnie," then without pausing as though resigned to the fact, "why are you not at home serving your husband's dinner instead of serving ours? Poor fellow is probably tired of getting his own meals when he has a wife. You'd best pack your things right away. We'll send for George. I want you to go home with him and be as good a wife to him as your mother has been to me."

Minnie, naturally overjoyed that her father seemed to accept her marriage, exclaimed, "I do love him, Father, and I was so afraid you and Mama would not have considered me old enough to marry him and that you would have tried to stop me." She rose from the table and embraced her father; he kissed her and turned away to dry his tears.

Minnie and her mother disappeared upstairs, while her brother Allen, much to his chagrin, was ordered to get George.

George arrived barely an hour later. He had been told only that Mr. McIntyre wished to see him immediately. Reining in the horse and buggy in the yard, Allen jumped down and scampered ahead to the house. For one insane moment George seriously considered turning about and galloping at full speed for the next county and might very well have done so if James hadn't emerged from the house. The fact that James appeared to be unarmed lessened George's intense terror only slightly. Minnie and her mother watched breathlessly from Minnie's bedroom as James strode purposefully towards George. Then he extended a rough, friendly hand which George eagerly grasped.

"Well, George, I'm so glad you've come; Elizabeth and I have just discovered that we have someone that belongs to you." At that, Minnie laughed aloud, her voice ringing out over the heavy night air. George looked up and could just make out his bride of two weeks waving energetically. Finally able to relax he too began to laugh.

When the wagon was packed and Minnie securely installed beside George, James wished them every happiness and sent them on their way. Then, turning quietly to his wife, he put his arm around her and walked with her to the kitchen door. The noisy clap of the screen door was followed almost immediately by a far noisier clap of thunder and brilliant bolt of lightning. The busy tapping on the roof began softly at first, then harder and harder as sheets of warm rain pelted furiously from the inky sky. James hugged Elizabeth just a little tighter and together they listened to the storm in wonder.

This was the beginning of married life for Daisy's parents. On hot midsummer evenings like that fateful one in 1885, Daisy, who was born March 13, 1891, often sat as a child with her mother on the front porch of their home in Peterborough and listened to the tale of how her beloved parents had met and secretly married, and of how her mother eventually came to live with her father and start their home.

Minnie often said, "Now, Daisy, it was a very foolish thing for a girl of sixteen to run off and marry secretly; I ought to have told my mother and father what I was planning. I hope you will always come to me and tell me about your important plans so we can talk about them." As Daisy nodded off to sleep in her mother's loving arms, she promised to seek her advice. In the many years that followed Daisy kept her promise and was always thankful she did, frequently thinking how curious it is that promises lightly made are often solemnly kept and those propped up with great ceremony and reverence are often lightly (and tragically) broken.

Daisy was nine years old when her grandfather died. He had been very kind and tender towards her and when her mother told her of his death, she understood that she would no longer be able to look forward to his visits and listen to his stories of foreign wars and far-off places. She felt a loss, but scarcely grief. The funeral made a great impression on little Daisy. It took place in October—a crisp, sparkling Monday afternoon ablaze with autumn color. The whole occasion struck her as one of great pomp and circumstance and from the moment she entered the great dark church with its musty ecclesiastical atmosphere through which the ceremonious strains of the organ echoed, she was caught up in what she understood at the time to be a great drama.

Her grandfather was a military man and had belonged to the Church of England, but the family were faithful adherents of the local Christian and Missionary Alliance Church with its simple airy décor and large pleasant windows. The colorful scenes and figures in stained glass and the rainbows that cast their rays of color into the gloomiest corners of the sanctuary fascinated Daisy as did her grandfather lying motionless and white.

Later, in the churchyard she watched with wide-eyed wonder and amazement all the strange and somber proceedings around the graveside and felt oddly soothed by the droning voice of the presiding cleric. In the future she attended many funerals, and often searched the faces of young children gathered around the grave, wondering what thoughts must be racing through their heads as they were witnessing the mystical pageant typical of funerals.

The casket was draped with the flag, on top of which was placed the great bearskin hat that her grandfather had worn in the army, and beside that, his sword. It was all very impressive and quite mysterious to her then.

After the graveyard ceremonies were over, Daisy and her family rattled along in the hired carriage, turning finally into their familiar street. She felt a great sense of relief that the afternoon had ended and the drama concluded. Something about the whole scene that autumn deeply disturbed her. It could have been the tears and anguished look of utter helplessness in her mother's eyes as she stood over grandfather's grave. Daisy had always been certain that her mother had complete control over all evil forces that could ever harm her and to see her so grief-stricken tended to shake the girl's childish security.

Daisy looked forward to Sunday mornings. It was a happy day in the house—a time of being together and going to church. Sunday meant that her father would be with them all day. This was especially important to her brother Cress, the elder boy, surrounded as he was by the women of the family most of the time. Cress was clever, but never applied his mind to schoolwork as diligently as Daisy. Although two years her senior, he was, to her great dismay, in the same class at school, and never heeded her frequent pleading with him to study his lessons. Perhaps she was less concerned about Cress's future and more about the shame she thought his academic failures brought upon the family. Despite her annoyance at his constant disregard of her warnings, she could not resist his winsome manner and sparkling wit and Cress always managed to reduce her to hysterical laughter just when she was trying the hardest to reprimand him most severely for his errant ways. Whenever he was around, the house seemed filled with sunshine. Cress proved in later years that all Daisy's concern for him was quite unnecessary for he became an outstanding businessman and a brother of whom she could be proud.

The highlight of any Sunday was centered around the church, which was strongly evangelical and placed great emphasis on missionary work. Daisy carefully chose her Sunday attire and always laid it out on the chair in the room that she shared with Violet, her oldest sister. The family lived very modestly and so Daisy had little from which to choose, but she was persuaded that the importance of the occasion merited much thought. Everything of course had to match properly and coordinate, even if it was just a bit of ribbon or lace.

Violet found Daisy's Saturday night deliberations a great source of amusement. Her sparkling, deep black eyes would follow her sister as she spread her simple dress on the bed and tried first this ribbon, then that, pondering at length over each.

"Oh, Daisy!" she would exclaim, laughing and tossing her beautiful dark curls, "you're so very particular." Then wrapping the bedclothes about her, she would swirl about the room mockingly. "M'lady would like more lace?"

Although Daisy loved Violet very much, she became upset with her at times like this. She thought her too carefree, and Violet thought Daisy not carefree enough. What frustrated Daisy most was that Violet apparently mistook her care for vanity, which it was not, for Daisy gave little thought, perhaps too little, to the impression she made upon others. On the contrary, she felt that Sunday morning was a time of great importance and therefore required special attention to things like dress to set it apart from other mornings.

Perhaps Daisy was a little jealous of Violet's open, cheerful disposition, her stunning appearance, and, later, her great attractiveness to many boys, and failed to recognize her good-natured jests as attempts to mollify her usually serious, contemplative nature.

The Sunday following her grandfather's funeral was particularly welcome. Daisy's home, usually cheerful and bright, had been very somber that week. Even Cress sensed his mother's grief, and had been humorless and quiet. Grandmother McIntyre, left alone, had come to live with the family. That Sunday morning she was wearing a long, simple black dress with a high lace collar, a style she usually wore even many years later. She had a great spirit; although she had come to their home to be comforted, she seemed to give far more comfort that she received. She loved beautiful poetry and could recite long portions from the works of the great poets of her day. No matter what happened in the home she always had a proverb that would fit the situation perfectly.

Several times that week, Daisy had come upon her mother and grandmother softly praying, unaware of her presence. In the following years her grandmother stayed with them when she was not visiting with her other daughter and Daisy often saw her praying with her mother. As she later became aware, they prayed for her. Daisy drew great strength from her grandmother until she was taken home many years later just before her ninety-eighth birthday.

After breakfast, the family set off for church. Daisy's father and mother walked with her grandmother. Violet and Cress skipped ahead with Hazel, who was a year younger than Daisy. Hazel was as fun-loving as Violet and shared Cress's clever wit. Daisy thought their frivolity unbecoming for a Sunday morning and so she walked quietly behind with her youngest sister, Ruth, who toddled along clasping Daisy's hand tightly. Although she was almost three, Ruth was painfully shy and very rarely spoke without the greatest encouragement. She was an exceptionally clever little girl even at such a young age, and had a sense of propriety and diligence.

The Billings family filled an entire pew. Daisy, observing her mother, father and grandmother, bowed her head reverently during prayers, sang lustily during hymns, and stumbled eagerly across the pages of the King James when the Scripture was being read. But it was the sermon she looked forward to the most—quite unusual for a young child. Dr. Zimmerman, whose name she could pronounce only with difficulty until she was seven, was a large, robust, distinguished-looking man with a full, pleasant voice, and she loved to hear him speak.

That morning, Daisy sat spellbound as he preached. She recalled later that he said God had set a high standard which one could never expect to reach in his own strength. Left to his own abilities, man must fail. But, Dr. Zimmerman went on to say, if people realized their sin and error and asked the forgiveness of God, receiving

Jesus His Son as personal Savior, salvation would be theirs, and they could have the assurance of being with God when the time came for them to leave this world.

She had heard this message often before, but the events of the last week now began to bring its true meaning into focus. She was scarcely aware of Ruth's little hand tugging at hers as she trotted breathlessly beside her. All of her bitterness towards her brothers and sisters and intolerance of them weighed heavily upon her. When she reached home, she was deeply convicted even at this early age of nine.

That afternoon, she approached her mother alone in the parlor. Deeply disturbed, she said, "Mother," in barely audible voice, "if it had been me, not Grandfather, who died last week, how could I be certain that I would have gone to heaven?"

At first her mother said nothing. It was one of those poignant moments in both of their lives when nothing needed to be said at all. She smiled as sweetly as Daisy ever remembered any human smile. In Daisy's childish, troubled eyes her mother at that instant appeared to be an angel. Her halo of soft hair was like fine gold. Daisy could see her own tortured countenance reflected in her mother's lustrous eyes. Her hand, though roughened from ceaseless toils, tenderly caressed Daisy's cheek to collect the salty tears that gathered there.

Many of her mother's faithful prayers were answered in that instant. Time was frozen for Daisy like a great divide separating the darkness of her childish pride and selfish ways from rebirth in the light of God's grace and forgiveness. Perhaps her mother grasped the joyful knowledge that the prayer she must have repeated so many times need never again be uttered. Her supplications would now be that Daisy might find a place of useful service among God's children. Her mother's momentary pause in responding to Daisy's question rendered it rhetorical. Other voices rushed into her mind, speaking the great truths of salvation from the Word of God—Scriptures she had heard, read and memorized in her Peterborough childhood, the Word becoming flesh and now dwelling within her. The Word which she now believed seemed like a great net into which she hurled her childish trust.

Then her mother spoke clearly and simply, "Daisy, the Bible says in John 5:24, 'Verily, verily' (which means 'truly'), 'I say unto you.'" She landed upon the pronoun *you* emphatically, then paused dramatically and finished "'He that heareth my word and believeth on Him that sent me hath everlasting life.' That means you have it now, if you believe on the Lord Jesus Christ."

Nothing more was said just then. Daisy retired from the parlor and climbed the stairs to her room, feeling as if she were climbing a staircase to heaven. She was as certain that God was now waiting at the end of her life, whenever it might come, as she was that her own tiny room with its familiar security waited to welcome her at the top of the stairs.

Looking back years later at that happy autumn day, Daisy marveled that so few human words were spoken. Her mother, whose knowledge of Scripture, wisdom and judgment were so abundant, uttered but a few simple sentences. When people feel they need a special gift to lead a soul to Christ, one cannot help but think of conversions similar to Daisy's, the conviction under which the Spirit of God brought her little heart, the brokenness wrought in her, and the great illumination and blessed peace the Spirit gave her in recognition of her timid faith. Such blessed gifts—all hers, the result of just a few words spoken.

It remained a mystery to Daisy that she had found Christ at such an early age and was spared so many years floundering in wretched darkness and miserable separation from God, like some who are often totally unaware of their true condition. By finding Christ young in life, she not only had an eternity to look forward to where she would be forever safe with Him, but she also had enjoyed a long and satisfying journey through the world as His child. She concluded that the short time spent here in this world is of little consequence in comparison with an eternity spent in the glory of God's presence. However, this knowledge did little to alleviate Daisy's distress at seeing dear souls who come to Christ tormented by the specter of a wasted life. Whatever the cause of her inclusion in that category of youthful converts, its effect was that almost immediately she felt the strain of a great responsibility to use her life as God would have her do—to the profit of His kingdom. She did not look upon this responsibility as a strain in the sense that one feels burdened or fatigued, but rather as the pleasant, exciting strain a well-toned athlete feels in that instant before the starting gun—invigorated, full of hope, unimpeded by the rigors, pains and pitfalls of the course that lies ahead.

Daisy thought many times about the fascinations of Christian conversion and the diversity of experiences and feelings that seem to accompany it. For some it is a moment of exceptionally intense emotion, often accompanied with bitter tears or bubbling exhilaration, evident to any dispassionate observer. Others undergo a quiet, but marvelous illumination, which may go almost undetected by all except the one who has been converted. And, of course, there is a whole range of experiences between these apparently extreme cases, all genuine, all in their way memorable.

Unfortunately, the terms *to be converted* and *to be saved* in modern parlance have taken on a meaning suggestive of an emotionally-charged response. This is unfortunate because both of these terms—given their proper meaning—express, as well as the severe limitations of language will permit, the truth of what happened to Daisy that Sunday afternoon in 1899.

For her "to be saved" always captured the negative aspect of that moment, evoking as it does the terrible and awesome evil from which she was spared; "to be converted" suggests the positive features of the Christian life characterized by radical change, the passing of old things and the newness of life which accompanies rebirth in Christ. While "conversion" and "salvation" may regrettably be imperfectly understood by most of the population nowadays, Daisy was comfortable with these terms as adequately descriptive of her basically indescribable first personal encounter with the living Lord.

A second absorbing mystery of Christian conversion and salvation which Daisy felt was the all-too-common waning of that first burst of sheer joy and exuberant zeal to be all God expects of His children. Like a newborn infant announcing his arrival with a thunderous, inarticulate howling, seemingly far more vocal than his tiny frame would allow, the babe in Christ wants to make his presence known and rejoice aloud in celebration of his new-found faith. Then, as days stretch to weeks, months and years, that initial passion fades, renewed again only intermittently. When in later life Daisy met Christian servants laboring in scores of places, doing hundreds of tasks, it always seemed to her that the most effective work was carried on, not by the most intelligent, the richest, or the best educated, but by those most consistently passionate in the things of God.

Daisy shared in this "lukewarmness" of so many Christians, but was no less normal in her early response to conversion. It was a memorable time in her life, enlivened by abounding joy and inner peace and characterized by a compelling desire to please God in her living. She often regretted the times she had pressed Cress too severely on what she considered to be his failings or had too eagerly cast a bitter, reproachful first stone at Violet and Hazel. On those occasions, gripped by remorse she had tried to assuage her conscience by asking for their forgiveness. But in the glow of her first personal experience with divine grace (though just a little girl of nine), she felt more deeply the awfulness of her sin and longed to set the record straight with each member of her family—to start afresh, as it were, with a clean slate.

Cress was caught quite off guard. Probably he had not the slightest idea what evil acts Daisy had committed which she now implored him to forgive, heaping heartfelt apologies upon his already spinning head. In her anxiety to clean her slate, she failed to realize that Cress, who was himself a child of God, was possessed of a gentle and tender nature which no doubt had not only forgiven but easily forgotten her transgressions, no matter how recently they may have occurred. Cress bore no grudges. In any event he mercifully forgave her. Perhaps he was even a little apprehensive, so repentant was her manner, that he was releasing her from some hitherto undetected, but nonetheless troublesome sin.

When she was sure of his forgiveness, she told him of her decision to accept Jesus, whereupon the cloud of confusion evaporated from his brow as though he now fully understood her unusual behavior. Cress was obviously pleased and Daisy felt him more a brother than she had thought possible. Many, many years later when dear Cress lay wasted at the end of his life, his body mercilessly riddled with cancer and his breathing heavy and uneven, Daisy would visit him in his sick room. She loved those visits and the warmth and good cheer that emanated from him. His irrepressible humor and twinkling eyes far exceeded the brilliance of the many sprays of spring flowers scattered around him. He was far happier, far more content, his face more luminous than any of the long, drawn, gray faces of the relatives and friends who gathered round him, speaking in velvet tones and somber syllables.

His cheerful spirit followed Daisy doggedly all her life, never allowing her to weep or sorrow more than she ought. As she watched him slip gently away, she thought fondly of his readiness to forgive her and his intolerance of any rift between them so long ago as she, a babe in Christ, witnessed for her Lord first to Cress. She remembered watching life ebb from his body and praying silently at his bedside that God would renew in her even then the spirit of tender forgiveness she cherished so in Cress.

Daisy's experience with Violet and Hazel put her new-found faith to a greater test than the encounter with her easy-going brother. After some searching, she found them huddled together under the cellar stairs, engrossed in a game of checkers, which, of course, was strictly forbidden on Sundays in the Billings' household, just as indulging in games of any kind was in many Victorian homes. Looking back, it seemed to her that Violet and Hazel were not at all fond of checkers, much preferring more active and daring pursuits. She could conclude only that the possibility of being found out added an invisible dimension of danger to the game which made it more like crossing the Trent River on a raft during spring run-off than the thoughtful game it appeared to be.

Daisy's appearance brought looks of disappointment to her sisters' faces. They no doubt thought that they would now be compelled to bargain with her to keep her from telling their parents. They would rather have been caught by their mother, if caught at all, and had it out with her on the spot. Daisy had sometimes broken her pledge of silence to them in an unguarded moment (often weeks after the event).

She immediately launched into an earnest plea for their forgiveness for any injury she might have caused them, promising to be more tolerant of their behavior in the future. They were, of course, delighted with her penitence and testimony. They were especially happy for the miraculous way Daisy's timely conversion had spared them punishment. They were sure now that she would not disclose this gross sin to their mother. She left them hunched over, the board supported between them on their knees, once more engrossed in strategy and no doubt greatly relieved that she could be trusted to protect them. She was only vaguely aware of having been used but it was of no real concern to her at the time. She felt that the record was set straight and she could make a new beginning.

Not long afterwards Daisy learned a very important, but hard lesson. Aunt Vera, her father's sister, was an actress. She had been on the stage in England and New York and was visiting in Peterborough between her acting engagements. She enjoyed taking Daisy and her sisters to buy pretty clothes, and asked Daisy what she would like. Daisy said that she had always wanted a beautiful hat covered with ostrich plumes to wear to church.

Daisy was rather young to sport a hat like this but after shopping all over Peterborough, they found her heart's desire, and when Sunday morning rolled around, Daisy wore her charming hat to church. She felt very elegant, but, to her dismay, when she came out of church a very wet snow was falling and she knew her feathers would go limp and be ruined forever. She watched all the stylish, opulent ladies getting into their covered carriages. How she wished a carriage would pull up for her! To her great surprise a carriage drew up right in front of her and since no one seemed to be using it, Daisy mounted the steps as if she owned it and asked the driver to take her home.

As she rode along, she felt more like a lady than she ever had. She might have been a princess. She was so proud and happy. Just as her fantasies peaked, she turned her head to one side and got a glimpse of her family plodding sourly, soaked to the skin. Her father looked up and caught sight of her. His face went white with rage. Daisy did not dare ask the driver to stop, because she was terrified of what her father might say. He had such a quick temper and so far he had not learned to control it.

When she reached home, she gave the driver all the money she had, and trembling, went into the house to await the arrival of the family. Her father was livid; shaking a finger at her, he said, "You, young lady, are to put that fancy hat away and never wear it again! I do not want you to become so proud that you cannot walk home with your family just because of that hat!"

Daisy's young heart was broken for the moment. She felt this was a cruel punishment and most unnecessary. Slowly she walked up to her room, took one last longing look at her pride and joy, and carefully and with great finality placed it on the shelf in her clothes cupboard. Sitting down on the bed she wept softly to herself as she bowed her head and asked God to help her get over this deep hurt and forgive her if she was proud. As she prayed, the Lord seemed to say, "It could have been worse. It is only a hat. Your father might have said you could not go to church anymore, Daisy." From that experience long, long ago, Daisy felt that her heavenly Father was trying to teach her a truth—that material things are not important. They can be swept away at any time, but eternal things can never be taken away. Daisy never wore that hat again and the wonderful part of it was, she lost all desire to wear it. She reasoned that it must have been bought for her by her Aunt Vera to teach her a very important truth, although neither of them knew that at the time.

As time went on Daisy's little faith began to grow. She looked forward to Sunday more than ever before, taking less and less interest as the weeks went by in the activities that had been so important to her in the past. Naturally she attended morning services, but soon she began to go to Sunday school each Sunday afternoon and services at night. Though she pressed each member of her family to join her, they were often dissuaded by the weather as the winter months drew on. The days became ever shorter; bitter winds and swirling snowfalls held Peterborough in an icy grip.

Their home was on the outskirts of town, and not well protected from the winter weather. The shortest route to church crossed a farmer's field and then went along a lovely stretch of country road which often totally vanished under the snows blown by the howling winds. Daisy made it her invariable practice to trudge, often alone, three times each Sunday along that lonely route, and yet, not alone at all. Though she was fearful in the dark or alone at night, she seemed to be completely unconcerned on those particular journeys.

An image of Jesus, pictured as He so often is, with soft brown hair and warm hazel eyes, walked with her, His great warm cloak engulfing her, shutting out the fury of the storm, calming all her fears. Never had she experienced such security and comfort as she felt crossing that field in winter and finding her way down the country road amidst ever changing drifts. Often, with no path ahead, she was conscious of His presence. On these occasions she would break into some familiar hymn or chorus. Her tiny voice was soon whisked off to mingle with the fury of the storm and vanish somewhere high in the tempestuous heavens. Such exhilaration was hers! Such inexpressible joy!

Finally she would come upon the church, sending forth a warm glow, and here she joined a handful of faithful saints in praise and worship. Her mother's duties in the home made it difficult for her to accompany Daisy, but she did, of course, as often as possible.

One such night in February came often to mind years later. During a particularly severe blizzard, Daisy and her mother were crossing the field. She could see her mother tremble with every frigid gust and Daisy told her that she would make room for her inside Jesus' cloak. She understood readily, and little Daisy thought her mother could feel His presence too—she seemed more content after that as they pressed on together.

The drifts had so eliminated any trace of their usual path that they stayed close to the fence, almost feeling their way along. Without warning, her mother faltered, tumbling into the snow. Pulling Daisy down on top of her, she cried, "Oh, Daisy! we've stumbled on a dead cow!" Daisy concluded that she was quite right as the three of them lay in the snow, her mother struggling to regain her feet and Daisy horror-stricken at the prospect of sharing a snowbank with the unfortunate and decidedly dead beast, apparently frozen quite stiff. Her mother was standing beside her again and pulling her up; they vigorously brushed each other's clothes and started off more cautiously. Daisy's momentary terror, evaporating in the face of her mother's placid response to the whole episode, was replaced by a strange sense of grief.

Without the constant guiding care of Jesus, Daisy thought, surely she would be as lost and utterly abandoned, as likely to stumble and not get up as the hapless cow. As her mother tugged her along, Daisy turned her head for one last look but the drifts had already covered the frozen carcass.

Of course after Daisy's conversion she continued to do things which she knew she ought not to do. But now she felt conscience-stricken and penitent on realizing she had failed in some aspect of Christian living. She was unable to avoid temptations as they stole into her life.

Sometimes she left her bed in the middle of the night, having prayed earnestly for God's forgiveness for some wrong she had done to her brother or sisters. She sought out and awakened the one whom she had injured to ask forgiveness, which was always readily granted by them, no doubt in hope that she would leave them to resume their rudely disturbed slumber. Daisy was unable to rest comfortably without this kind of absolution. She was extremely grateful to them for the stoicism with which they endured her nocturnal visits. They would often lie in their beds reviewing their dealings with her during the day to determine whether she might be expected during the night to seek forgiveness for some slight or thoughtless word. Each of them, even little Ruth, was most tolerant of this particular eccentricity.

Daisy did not always confine her visitations to confessionals. Often she felt a great urgency at any hour to impress upon Cress, Violet, Hazel, or Ruth (or some combination) some vital message. When she was twelve, Dr. Zimmerman gave a series of prophetic messages which greatly impressed her. He concluded with a stirring message on the reign of the Antichrist, and the necessity of resisting the mark of the Beast. Daisy was persuaded that Hazel would not be prepared to resist the mark and ventured from her bed in the night to creep unnoticed to Hazel's room. Shaking Hazel vigorously until she was wide awake, Daisy told her she must promise never to accept the mark of the Beast under any circumstances no matter what was threatened against her. Hazel didn't seem to share Daisy's intense concern and rolled over, assuring her somewhat too casually that she would decline the dreaded mark when the time came to do so.

On many silent nights Daisy lay awake thinking about her life and what might become of it. Still just a little girl she could not understand why she bickered with her young friends and family and did things she knew displeased God. If she was a Christian, she thought surely her conduct should be different. Yet, she sinned willfully, again and again. Then she prayed in a faltering, clumsy way and for many months after her conversion sought God's face.

The answer to this dilemma came in a most unspectacular way, but Daisy never forgot the enormous impact this tiny incident had on her life. Her mother was busy preparing dinner one evening and Daisy, along with Cress, Violet and Hazel, gathered around the kitchen table to do their lessons. Her mother, stoking the fire in the stove, asked if one of them would go to the woodshed and bring in more wood. This touched off a storm of feeble excuses. Each of them selfishly determined that someone else was better suited for the task. In the midst of their bitter exchanges, Daisy heard the Holy Spirit speaking to her in clear, unmistakable terms: "You go, Daisy; it will take only a few minutes and then it will be all done; the quarreling will be over and the victory yours."

Quickly she left for the woodshed. The storm subsided. Although this was just a seemingly small, insignificant incident Daisy ever after regarded that moment as the first victory in her life over temptation. She thought of it as the first time she experienced the power which the Holy

Spirit makes available and as the beginning of a yielding to the Spirit's control. This yielding to the Spirit brought then, as it did many times since, great joy flooding her heart.

Daisy had accepted Christ as Savior. She knew what it was to have His Spirit controlling her life, and now, under the guidance of her mother, Daisy took the third great step in her budding Christian life.

The baptismal service had been scheduled for a Friday night in March and Daisy made it plain that she meant to be a candidate. That morning, her mother caught her arm as she hurried off to school. She tucked a note in Daisy's coat pocket. "Show this to your teacher, Daisy, and she will let you leave school early. I made an appointment for you to see Dr. Zimmerman about your baptism tonight; so you must go straight to his home from school."

At three o'clock, Daisy found herself standing before the great oak door of the manse, very nervous indeed about her first personal meeting with the man who had so influenced her brief life and of whom she had a kind of awe. The door opened and immediately her fears scattered before the broad, ruddy, smiling face welcoming her. Putting his strong hand gently upon her shoulder, Dr. Zimmerman ushered her into his study and helped her into one of the overstuffed chairs. Daisy, feeling very small, nestled comfortably into one corner of that monstrous chair, her legs thrust straight forward, with no hope of ever reaching the intricate worn pattern of the exotic Victorian carpet spread beneath her. Her head was barely visible above the upholstery engulfing her.

She scrutinized the room with wide-eyed wonder, starting with the numberless volumes covering at least two-thirds of the wall space. They were guarding, she decided, virtually all the knowledge which man had managed to accumulate and record since being expelled from the garden. Her gaze passed to the cluster of degrees and diplomas surrounded by tiers of books (like a flock gathered safely in its fold), resplendent with ornate, unintelligible script and slightly faded crimson ribbons with officious red seals.

Daisy looked at the great desk set like a pillar in one corner of the room, overflowing with papers scattered about amidst open books, giving her the distinct impression she had intruded upon the preparation of one of those marvelous sermons which so enthralled her. Finally her eyes came to rest upon his beaming face enlivened by the contagious twinkle of his great blue eyes, as he sat in the chair directly opposite her.

"Well, Daisy," he announced with pleasant gruffness, "your mother tells me that you wish to be baptized tonight. Why?"

"Because everyone must know beyond any doubt that I am a Christian." Daisy was somewhat taken aback at the boldness and speed of her answer to a question that perhaps was calculated to evoke a more complex and thoughtful response. But Dr. Zimmerman seemed well pleased and for the next hour he led her through the scriptural teaching on baptism and finally prayed with her. Daisy took all of this to be an unparalleled privilege.

That evening Daisy was the smallest one to go through the waters of baptism in front of the entire congregation, which included, to her infinite joy, her entire family.

As she emerged from the water, Dr. Zimmerman's

familiar voice quoted John 5:24, "Verily, verily, I say unto you, he that heareth my word and believeth on Him that sent me hath everlasting life," and Luke 12:8, "Whoever shall confess me before men, him shall the Son of man also confess before the angels of God."

The joy she had felt in confessing Jesus before her family only months before now multiplied as she affirmed her faith in the presence of so many. Reflecting on her own baptism confirmed in her mind that all the precious moments of private illumination and contact with the Lord must be balanced by some form of public statement of faith, of which baptism was for her the most memorable and significant. She was quite sure that to those who witnessed her baptism no visible sign of destiny or divine providence was evident. They saw only a rather nervous little girl emerging from the murky waters, squinting, gasping and noisily sucking life-restoring air. Although disheveled and dripping, Daisy felt the everlasting arms bearing up her spirit as clearly as Dr. Zimmerman's arms bearing up her body—it was perfect security.

The spring of 1900 dawned upon the world with a special sense of hope. The future was full of promises of prosperity, technological blessings untold and peace without end (as soon as the unruly Boers could be persuaded to accept the inevitability of the British Empire). Daisy was unaware of these utopian prognostications. For her that spring had infinitely more precious blessings and hope, which only one's first spring as a child of God can bring, an awareness and illumination heightened by the rebirth with which God surrounded her as she went to and from school and church, carrying on her everyday life in Peterborough.

Of course, all the promises of the world that spring were not fulfilled. Brave words revisited mockingly as the years passed. The coming century was to stagger in two world conflicts, and numberless, interminable wars of national liberation—all with no victor, only vanquished, liberating no one, except perhaps those who died before realizing the cruel irony of apparent victory. Poverty and starvation were to increase as the poor grew ever poorer, the rich ever more unhappy, grasping hopelessly at cars, vacations, homes, education, and ultimately popping pills of every hue which promised relief from undesirable annoyances, unhappiness, despair, boredom, idleness, and eventually even childbirth.

"How fortunate I was that spring," thought Daisy, "that I put my trust, my childish hope in promises which were unfailingly realized in passing years, that I established my embryonic faith in Him who stilled the storms that tried vainly to obliterate permanently the pathway before me." Her faith was in Him who fulfills the promise of peace in pandemonium.

In years to come Daisy saw unmitigated selfishness revered, self-satisfaction in the guise of happiness pursued everywhere, knowledge and its use without wisdom or morality universally endorsed, sensual excess the new spirituality, childbirth avoided at the most astounding and as yet unrealized cost. While the popular understanding of the meaning of life was reversed as totally and violently as the Fundy tides, Daisy, looking back, was stunned that God should have sunk her heart into the sands of His love at such a tender age, like an anchor plowing ever deeper as the current builds against it.

The strikingly different seasons came and went in Peterborough, and with them the years. Strangely, Daisy remembered little of those years, except that they were abundantly happy for her, perhaps the most contented of her life. Trips across the field and down the country road to church continued with greater frequency. She longed to attend meetings whenever they were held, especially the women's prayer meeting at which she first learned with some uneasiness to pray publicly in the presence of many women years her senior from the towns and farms in the district.

Cress still felt the sting of her proddings but they had little effect. Her sisters still endured her warnings on the necessity of taking life more seriously and applying themselves more assiduously to their lessons. Daisy often watched as they sat nervously chattering in the kitchen on some crisp winter afternoon, straining as they laced their well-worn skates, awaiting the arrival of their current boyfriends. When the boys arrived, also skate-shod, they would all walk precariously, wobbling their way down to the canal nearby, gossiping energetically and laughing contagiously as one would tumble headlong in the snow. Daisy observed their progress from her bedroom window from which she had a clear view.

They reminded her of four decrepit, elderly paupers as they struggled uncertainly down to the canal, clutching each other for support, their ankles trembling as the clumsy blades would catch in a rut or slip out from under them without warning. Then magically as they reached the edge of the frozen surface, they would be transformed into graceful, gliding, balletlike creatures, swirling and spinning enchantingly. They reminded Daisy of transformed cripples emerging from the Bethsaida pool, their joyful voices ringing out over the bleached countryside. In later life that childhood scene was to Daisy a picture of many Christians stumbling along on earth in a strange environment, like travelers in a foreign land, falling, clutching each other for stability on a slippery road. "We shall be transformed at the end of our faltering journey," she thought, "taking wings and rising up in graceful flight, at last to fulfill the role for which we were made, praising and serving Jesus in perfect coordination."

As Daisy rarely entertained boys, she felt some envy perhaps at her sisters' unfailing ability to shut out all the unhappy, tragic things in life and frolic endlessly with apparent contentment and joyfulness. But she also ardently wished that they could share with her the burden which seemed to rest uneasily upon her as with passing years she felt a vague and undefinable compulsion to render some service to God, which would to the tiniest degree be worthy of the enormous love she knew He had for her. So in the quietness and peace of the southern Ontario countryside, God was leading yet another step along the path He had planned.

At the age of seventeen, Daisy was in her final year of school. She was feeling much more strongly now the call of God but could find no outlet for it. Just as she was beginning to think that her life might after all end in Peterborough (no doubt on one of the frequent trips across the farmer's field and down the country road, perhaps to join the frozen cow upon which her mother and she had stumbled seven years before), without having served at all, she heard from one of the elderly ladies in her church about Nyack.

This lady described a Bible school in Nyack, New

York, where Daisy could study to become a missionary in some, as she envisioned it, exotic and remote heathen land. Preoccupied with this thought, Daisy returned one day from school to find her brother Cress seated in a state of utter despair at the kitchen table. She had never seen his usually beaming face so troubled.

"Daisy," he said, holding back tears, "the doctor is upstairs with Mother and I don't know what is wrong with her. You'd better go up and—"

Suddenly, he was interrupted by an infant's shrill howling. Daisy rushed brusquely by Cress and climbed the stairs, arriving breathlessly at the top to discover that God had given them a new and vocal baby brother. Of course she knew that her mother was pregnant, and had been a little concerned, her pregnancy coming ten years after the birth of Ruth and rather late in her childbearing life. Once satisfied that her mother and the baby were both all right, Daisy returned to the tormented Cress, who was, even for a Victorian youth, hopelessly naive.

"Cress," she exclaimed, "Mother has given us a brand new baby brother!"

Cress just stared vacantly, turned snow white and dropped to the kitchen floor with a dull thud, fainting dead away.

Donald, the newest addition to the Billings household, was spoiled and Daisy had to bear a great part of the responsibility for that. Nothing pleased her more than to care for him, her mother being busy with so many household duties. Daisy pulled him in his go-cart about the neighborhood and vainly showed him off to any who could bear her prideful chatter. Often she packed a little lunch and took him for long walks for most of the day, pausing usually in the quietness of the local cemetery to let him eat.

One such occasion remained vividly in her memory. As they were sitting in the shade of a great maple, Donald was ravenously downing his egg sandwich. A funeral procession drew up not far away, and Daisy watched curiously to see if she could recognize any of the tear-stained faces of the mourners. Donald seemed to disregard this spectacle and Daisy thought him deeply engrossed in his lunch when suddenly his little voice intruded upon her dispassionate observations.

"It's so sad, isn't it, Daisy?" He was only two and did not understand sorrow, but he obviously felt it more than she did just then. Embarrassed, Daisy agreed that it was very sad indeed; she made haste to collect their things and pull Donald home.

Having now decided to go to Nyack at the first opportunity, Daisy thought of little else. But the months hurried on and school drew quickly to a close. She was painfully aware that her family had only enough money to maintain the home, and little was left of her father's pay for travel, education, or anything which was generally regarded as nonessential. So few of her friends and acquaintances had even finished high school that it was unthinkable to even consider asking her father for the money needed to continue her education at Nyack. Of course, at that time it was not regarded as advisable for a girl to go beyond high school. By June of that year (1907), Daisy felt despair again creeping upon her. Would she ever see Nyack or have the chance to serve the Lord in some remote mission field?

It was in this desolate state, her hopes crumbling ever

faster, that she returned one day from one of her outings with little Donald. He had seemed particularly tiresome that afternoon owing to Daisy's preoccupation with her own troubles. She hurried him off to his nap, rather roughly, almost resenting his cheerful resiliency in the wake of her impatience. Coming down to the parlor she found her father relaxing by the fire as he so often did on Sunday afternoons.

"Daisy," he said, a smile breaking across his face, "I expect since you are finishing school, you may be looking for a job. You'll be wanting money before long. I know you have some plans of your own." He paused to measure her reaction, but she, not quite sure what direction he was going in, just stared blankly. Then he continued, "Well, I spoke to one of our best customers at the mill and he said he would give you a job at his factory in town. You know the box factory down by the station?"

Suddenly, the cloud that had doggedly plagued Daisy for months was dissipated. She saw in her father's good news the chance she thought would never come. Instinctively she embraced him. He only chuckled and remarked, "I assume then you'll take the job."

Her father's assumption was quite correct and the following Monday found Daisy entering the employment office of the Peterborough Packaging Company to begin her first job. The factory was one of those great medieval stone structures with a multitude of tiny, grimy windows, only a few of which opened. It had two great smokestacks belching black clouds of smoke defiantly into the hazy summer atmosphere hanging over Peterborough. No one ever told Daisy what went into the boxes that were made at the factory, although that knowledge probably would not have made much difference to her at the time. The work was slow and boring. She passed the hours imagining what life would be like at Nyack and sometimes dreaming of where she might go after finishing her studies there—some tropic isle set in an emerald sea perhaps.

Her greatest delight was going to the bank to deposit her pay, calculating the balance yet to be collected and figuring out how many more weeks it would take before she could at last leave the box factory behind. She had decided she would stop work as soon as she had enough money in the bank to pay for her fare to Nyack, a few necessary items, and room and board for about two weeks. She estimated the handsome sum of sixty dollars would suffice. After that was exhausted, she was determined to rely on God to supply her day-to-day needs. Since she had obtained her job, it had never crossed her mind God would not always supply her needs.

With thirty dollars in the bank account, Daisy wrote to the Missionary Training Institute in Nyack, New York, later called Nyack College, and submitted her application for the following semester. It was accepted. The possibility of Nyack's rejecting her never entered her mind, so confident was she of the hand of God in this plan. Finally the great day arrived. Daisy had saved sixty dollars, enough to launch out on her long-awaited adventure.

2

Bible School Days

On the morning of Daisy's departure for Nyack, she was up earlier than anyone else in the house. On reflection, she thought it was probably more out of an unspoken longing to stretch her last moments in the only place she had ever lived, than out of a sense of excitement at the prospect of the adventure which lay before her. Since the time she first determined to go to Nyack she had thought of very little else, and not at all of the many things always taken for granted that would now be left behind.

Suddenly, on that chill October morning, the great flaming orb inching above the farmer's dazzling frosty field, so familiar to Daisy, seemed to illuminate much more than the sleeping Peterborough panorama. She glimpsed for the first time the enormous breadth of God's love and care for her. Born into a happy home in a pleasant, placid place, she had been taught early of God's wondrous grace and love for her. She saw the rich treasures that had been hers in Peterborough.

Dressing quietly, and confirming that Violet still slept soundly, she crept downstairs and out into the silent stillness of a frost-gripped dawn. Reaching the street, she turned and stood for several minutes, looking at the old house as if, by just holding her gaze upon it long enough, she could print it indelibly on her memory, like an early tintype that disappears but can be easily brought back again at will with a mere turn of the wrist to change the angle of reflection.

Daisy wished she could slip away then, never to face the farewells and wrenching separations she knew the day must hold. In today's world of seemingly endless travel and separation, it is difficult to visualize, much less comprehend, the great remorse that could in 1908 so easily overtake a seventeen-year-old girl leaving for the first time from her home and family in a small Ontario town.

At last Daisy turned and crossed the farmer's field to meet the country road leading down to the church. She paused a moment and then returned through the cemetery where little Donald had shared the mourners' sorrow, arriving before the house began to stir.

These were the experiences that impressed Daisy the most during her childhood and teen-age years. No doubt many things of seemingly gigantic importance at the time had faded from her memory and would be forever lost. That is one of the great inherent weaknesses which most of us share—complete inability, particularly in our youth, to recognize significant landmarks along the journey until long after we have passed them by, and worse, to mistake false landmarks for real ones.

Daisy rarely returned to Peterborough after that, preferring to remember it as it was that October morning of her departure, until much later in life when she was

drawn to the Peterborough lake district for a summer re-
treat with her own young family—an area to which her
children are still drawn as if by an invisible magnet. It was
never more resplendent than it was on that day with its
autumn colors, as if it were turning out its best to create a
picture she would always remember.

The train clattered along, threading its way past the
box factory exhaling darkly. At first many tracks and sid-
ings veered off in every direction; but the farther the train
rolled on, the fewer the rails and the faster the progress.
Every switch was thrown at just the right moment to direct
the train on the proper track until finally it was speeding
along on a single pair of rails bound for Toronto. Daisy
could think only of how she had been compelled at school
to memorize the names of the streets of Peterborough.

Daisy had always been impatient with and, to a certain extent, maddened by the "hot house" critics of Christian education. They argue that the protective environment of a Christian school has the undesirable effect of
insulating its students from the realities and vigors of the
real world and of depriving them of the right to freely
choose what creed to follow, and what faith to embrace.
The result is, they say, these students emerge from the
Christian school unprepared to contend with the evil
forces which abound on every side. They are sheep among
raving wolves.

In Daisy's experience, she had found the "hot house"
metaphor unconvincing. Her impression was that "hot
house" beginnings spawn the strongest plants. They have
a much lower mortality rate, and are far better equipped to
survive hostile environments than seedlings planted

among thorns. Yet, all through her life she noticed that the critics continued to multiply.

When Daisy's younger son, as pastor of The Peoples Church in Toronto, Canada, resolved in 1971 to establish a Christian elementary and secondary school, the "hot house" critics proved to be undiminished in numbers and zeal. Fortunately, the obviously apparent decay in some areas of public education and the powerful increase of evil in Canadian urban society persuaded a large number of Christian parents to support The Peoples Christian School, which enjoyed the blessing of God from its beginnings.

The parochial school revival in North America has not been motivated by a desire to escape exposure to evil in the world, which is always no further than the nearest television or theater, but rather, by Christian recognition of the imperative necessity to properly equip children and young people to contend with evil.

Everyone agrees that life is brief, but no one grasps the full meaning of this until years begin to pile up behind him. It was this comprehension, more than anything else, that persuaded Daisy of the importance of spending life to the greatest advantage of the kingdom of heaven. She realized if this meant she must pass up worldly pursuits, to which no doubt she might be attracted, in order to get on with the task to which she was called, then that was precisely what she must do. She knew that worldly experience would count for little after time had robbed her of the physical and mental capacities to do the thing which God would have her do. Therefore, Daisy never once regretted having attended a Christian school.

If it were possible to board a jet at the Peterborough

airport today, you could travel to and from Nyack in upper New York State many times in a day. Unfortunately you would miss the graceful, well-kept farms and stubbled fields of southern Ontario, the burgeoning of Toronto in 1908, the vista of an angry, deep blue, white-crested Lake Ontario from the deck of a brave little steamer and the welcome feel of firm, warm earth underfoot once again. You would also miss the meandering dusty roads winding through the gentle countryside of New York State to Nyack.

Experiencing travel for the first time, Daisy was full of excitement and breathless anticipation which she said was never equaled in all the longer and more exotic journeys she was to undertake many years later.

When she arrived at Nyack College back in 1908, it consisted of a small cluster of crude frame structures. Yet Daisy was not disappointed at the modest campus which was to be her home for the next three years. She regarded her enrolment at Nyack as a great privilege. It was the fulfillment of an ambition which had been her constant companion for several years past.

With the formalities of registration quickly completed, she was ushered to the dormitory by a severe, rotund woman who served as dean of women, and matron. Daisy followed her ample personage across the pleasantly treed grounds of Nyack until they came upon a large barnlike structure that gave the distinct impression of having been built for one purpose and, some considerable time later, having been converted to a wholly unrelated purpose. This was to be Daisy's new home.

Together they entered and climbed three flights of

rough stairs which groaned somewhat more under her companion's foot than her own. Arriving atop the last flight, the exhausted matron sighed heavily and struck out down the long hallway with a determined bearing, and Daisy struggled along behind her, clutching her humble suitcases. Arriving at the next to the last door on the right, the matron rapped heavily and the door flung open.

"Ada, greet your new roommate, Daisy," the matron barked, and pressed on into the room. It was not only beauty that attracted one to Ada Luce. She had an unforgettable manner and appearance that Daisy easily recalled to mind years later. Her long hair was pitch black, in contrast to her gray-blue eyes. She was, on first impression, pleasant in appearance, and, as Daisy soon discovered, excellent company. The matron stayed only long enough to verify that sheets and towels were adequately provided and then trudged heavily down the hallway. As her steps faded, Daisy turned to introduce herself more fully to Ada.

Ada came from an upper middle-class home in Toronto, and had never lacked for basic material comforts. Daisy was, of course, delighted to know she was Canadian, feeling, as she did, cut off from home and familiar things. That Ada was a gentle spirit was evident early in their friendship. She was not an activist, but more inclined to prayer and study. In the following weeks and months they prayed often together, Ada seemingly with effortless ease and Daisy always struggling. She came to greatly admire Ada's contemplative wisdom, a quality which she thought lacking in herself. Daisy discovered that friendships made at Christian schools can be very precious. These friendships are not mere matters of chance, for all the stu-

dents have come voluntarily, out of a greater or lesser degree of commitment, and are held together by a special
bond of love. Many of the friends Daisy cherished at Nyack
she never encountered again, and yet years later she
thought fondly of different ones, wondering what paths
God had opened for them.

Adelaide Pollard shared the room across the hall with
a student who was the most vocal occupant of the dormitory and had an endless repertoire of pranks and reserve
of energy to carry them out. By contrast, Adelaide was a
very sensitive soul who wrote moving verse. Daisy and
Ada met her that first afternoon at Nyack. She tapped
softly on their door, entering timidly, nervously clutching
several sheets of paper on which something had been
written in a tiny neat hand.

"I'm Adelaide Pollard. You must be Daisy Billings
and Ada Luce. I've just written a poem of dedication and I
wanted to share it with someone as we stand on the
threshold of a new school term." Ada and Daisy nodded
their approval and Adelaide began to read softly.

> Have Thine own way, Lord! Have Thine own way!
>   Thou art the Potter, I am the clay.
> Mold me and make me after Thy will,
>   While I am waiting, yielded and still.

She continued to recite several more verses, but
Daisy's mind was fixed on the searing meaning of that first
stanza. It came back to challenge her many times after she
first heard it. Years later the beautiful lyrics were set to
music and have been used extensively as a hymn of dedication.

Daisy had been at Nyack only several days when she

began to realize that her fortune was not likely to last much beyond the fall term. Of course student loans and grants were unknown during her school days. So, on Ada's advice, she made her way to the principal's office to discuss with him the sorry state of her finances. To her great astonishment, he suggested she take a part-time job.

All of the terrible memories of the box factory crowded her mind until the principal offered her a position in the school laundry, and she gratefully accepted it. The pay was extremely poor, even by contemporary standards, but at least one-half of her tuition was now secure. The other half and all her other needs were faithfully met in the succeeding weeks as she began to receive anonymous gifts from kind folk in Peterborough. How she wished she had known who her undisclosed benefactors were so she could tell them of the joy and thanksgiving to God their unflagging support brought to her soul.

Daisy, though convinced some of the girls came to Nyack to capture a husband, made it quite evident that her only purpose was to study and prepare for Christian service. Showing little, if any, interest in the more "eligible" boys, she found they soon rarely bothered with her. Consequently she often found herself in the company of some of the students who were less attractive physically, or less materially endowed. Ada many times teased her that she attracted "the lame, the halt, and the blind." This was doubtless an overstatement, but she did recall vividly one boy in particular who fitted Ada's description. Dick Stanley was tragically afflicted with a crooked spine and he moved around with greatest difficulty and in obvious discomfort. Daisy occasionally chatted briefly with him in the dining hall. Her sympathetic nature tried to show him special consideration as she thought his lot in life to be so unfair.

Soon after the commencement of the spring term, while sorting the laundry in preparation for washing, Daisy came upon a crumpled note tucked in the breast pocket of a shirt. Pulling it out and opening it gingerly, she began to read:

Dear Miss Billings,

I have enjoyed our talks together so much. I get such a blessing whenever I hear you pray aloud in chapel. The more I get to know you, the deeper my love for you grows. You are so tiny and dainty, and you have such a marvelous deep speaking voice. You are going to make a great preacher.

I think it is about time I told you that I am falling in love with you.

Affectionately,
Dick Stanley

Daisy stared at the note in astonished disbelief, completely unprepared for this unexpected development. It had never occurred to her that Dick felt anything beyond cordial friendship toward her. She decided to respond immediately. Sitting down amidst all the dirty laundry, in something less than a romantic setting, Daisy composed a reply that she later tucked into Dick's neatly ironed shirt. Just before she folded the note up and put it in the pocket, she read it over to make sure the message was clear:

Dear Mr. Stanley,

I received your note that you sent to me in the pocket of your shirt. I must tell you right away that I am not in love with anyone, and I don't want anyone to be in love with me just now. My only goal is to study God's Word, to be better equipped to preach it somewhere to those who have never heard. I have to devote all my time and energies to reaching my goal, and though I appreciate your kind thoughts of me, I am sure you will understand, and we shall continue to be good friends as we pray for each other.

In His service,
Daisy Billings

This ended her fleeting romance with Dick Stanley, the first of several equally brief romances punctuating her three years at Nyack.

The months stretched to years and by the spring of 1911, Daisy was facing the prospect of graduation from Nyack. With childhood and adolescent dreams quickly fading, she began to look seriously for some indication from God as to where He would have her serve. Although she had enjoyed her Bible school days and had many fond memories of them, she was anxious to move on to a place of active service.

A missionary from the West Virginia coal mines visited Nyack during Daisy's final semester and addressed the students one morning. Ada and Daisy were a little late arriving at chapel; the guest was already speaking as the girls opened the door of the chapel and slipped noiselessly inside. Daisy glanced around quickly to see if their late arrival had been noticed. Tardiness, especially where chapel was concerned, was frowned upon. However, everyone was listening with rapt attention. Then Daisy's eyes came to rest on the diminutive figure speaking in slow, deliberate tones, and barely visible behind the enormous pulpit. She was perhaps only in her fifties but very gray. Her face was tired and wan. Her whitened knuckles gripped the edge of the pulpit for support while she swayed continually from side to side as if trying to be seen from behind the ornate immensity of the lectern.

Daisy nudged Ada to take a seat in the last pew. The speaker's thin, willowy voice drifted across the motionless crowd of young students. Daisy strained to pick up the gist of her address.

They had heard several powerful speakers from time to time—voices charged with emotion, now in a high-pitched frenzy of animated gesticulation, now in a whisper drawing listeners to the edge of their seats. Their appeal was usually that the students consecrate their lives to full-time service for Jesus Christ. Each time they spoke, a wave of dedication swept the school. Daisy had always joined the others in avid determination to serve with renewed zeal the Master they all loved so deeply.

But somehow, this woman was different. Her strangely saddened face etched a life of suffering and hardship. Yet her eyes sparkled with determination and life. Yes, it was those eyes, dancing across the sanctuary, which spoke to Daisy, piercing her soul. As she listened she realized that this woman was not preaching at all. She was simply telling a story—her story.

She told them of the great need for preachers, doctors, and other Christian workers among the mountaineers of West Virginia. She described a rugged, hard place in which to work and stressed that if one did not feel fully dedicated to service, he would never be able to endure life in the mountains.

"If any of you are thinking of volunteering," she said, "you will have to forget your desires and do it for Jesus' sake because it is not an attractive place to serve. The need is great and I feel God has someone here today whom He is calling to this work."

After several verses of a hymn and a closing prayer, the students were dismissed. Daisy walked along in silence with Ada to the dormitory and climbed the stairs to their room. The closing words of the little gray-haired preacher echoed all around her—"To know God's will and not to do it is to be unfaithful." The real world around her grew dim and faded for those few moments into an obscure and irrelevant backdrop for her dreams. As she reached her room and opened the door, the lunch bell rang bringing her back to Nyack and Ada.

Finally, Ada, who had been silent, spoke. "You know, Daisy, we graduate in April. It's been three years. It seems more like three weeks to me. Where will you go when school is over?"

Daisy did not answer Ada right away, but reached for a biography that stood on the bookshelf. Out of this missionary biography dropped a little tract with a poem in it which Daisy read aloud:

> I said—"Let me walk in the fields,"
>   He said—"No, walk in the town."
> I said—"There are no flowers there."
>   He said —"No flowers, but a crown."
> I said—"But the skies are dark,
>   There is nothing but noise and din."
> And He wept as He sent me back—
>   "There is more," He said: "there is sin."
>
> I said—"I shall miss the light
>   And friends will miss me, they say."
> He answered—"Choose tonight
>   If I am to miss you, or they."
> I pleaded for time to be given,
>   He said—"Is it hard to decide?
> It will not be hard in Heaven
>   To have followed the steps of your guide."

Then into His hand went mine,
    And into my heart came He,
And I walk in a light Divine,
    The path I had feared to see.

George McDonald (1824–1905)

When she finished reading, the girls bowed their heads and committed their whole future to the Lord. They repeated the words of Adelaide's hymn, "Have Thine Own Way, Lord," and knew God was calling them to minister to the neglected mountaineers of West Virginia. Their young hearts responded to the call and they never looked back.

For those of us who have visited the beautiful mountain areas of West Virginia and have been impressed with the progress and sometimes affluence of the people, it is difficult to realize that at the turn of the century there were many places, both in the United States and Canada, that were quite primitive and very much like a "foreign" mission field.

3

Mountaineer Ministry

"Roaring Fork! Roaring Fork!" The conductor's boom-
ing announcement awakened Daisy from uneasy sleep.
She craned her neck to see past Ada, who still slept
soundly. This was Daisy's first glimpse of this little West
Virginia coal mining town tucked in the forgotten
mountain backwoods. The train threaded its way more
slowly for the final several miles of the long journey from
Nyack. A sea of ancient, well-worn mountains spread
endlessly into the purple mist rolling on more heavily on
each successive crest; primitive rough frame dwellings and
log cabins, each emitting a delicate wisp of smoke, were
scattered at random across the narrow valleys.

Daisy visualized herself with Ada as the sole inhabitants of one of these forlorn-looking homes. Would they
be lonely or frightened? Could they bear more separation
from home and family? Daisy tried to imagine what her
mother would be doing now as the distance between them
stretched ever farther. She could almost smell her
mother's homemade bread emerging from the old wood
stove in Peterborough. How curious, she thought, that
she should find herself in this place, pursuing an objective

so different from that of her brothers and sisters with whom she had shared a happy childhood!

Daisy glanced at her friend now just awakening. Ada had been determined that Daisy would not embark on this adventure alone, and, over the reservations of her family, Ada had volunteered with Daisy to go to the mountains. As Daisy thought how very fortunate she was to have such a loyal, dedicated companion, the little village came in view, a motley collection of shacks and rough-hewn structures. The dimming light of late afternoon added to the grayness and severity of the scene.

"Roaring Fork! Roaring Fork!" The train lurched and stopped, the locomotive hissing and spewing steam. Excitement peaked as the two weary travelers stepped onto the platform, wondering if anyone had been told of their arrival.

"You gals the missionaries we is expectin' from the Bible school?" a deep, gruff voice barked behind them. Daisy and Ada turned to face an enormous man who looked like someone from another world. His overalls were black with coal dust, and a tattered felt hat turned down all around almost meeting his grimy, matted beard completed his outfit. The girls nodded as he scrutinized them.

"I'm Joe. We heard you was comin' an' the folks 'round these parts sure are lookin' forward ta meetin' ya. Last missionary we had was an awful prim ole darlin'. Things is lookin' up, I reckon."

With that he roughly grabbed the cases and turned towards his wagon. The girls followed cautiously.

Rumbling along in Joe's decrepit wagon offered Daisy and Ada a chance to learn something about this, their first foreign mission field. Joe explained that the local residents had built a cabin to house any missionaries that could be persuaded to serve in this neglected area. Only occasionally was any professional medical assistance available. Education was haphazard, depending on how long the teacher could suffer the abominably overcrowded conditions in the tiny schoolhouse, which also served as a church when anyone cared enough to come.

Roaring Fork meant coal. Almost every adolescent and adult male worked in the mine. The miners' hours were long and life expectancies short. Life was generally cruel, marked by want of money, food, clothes, education—in short, want of all the things Ada and Daisy enjoyed from childhood. Contagious disease, particularly typhoid, spread almost unchecked and untreated, reaping its grim harvest. Families were generally large; children seemed to be everywhere as the wagon rolled along the dusty road, past rude cabins, dark and ominous, as if glowering at the awestruck missionaries.

Leaving the town behind, the road became more primitive. Ada felt the seeds of doubt spring up within her, as she was jolted by each successive rut and pothole. Could she survive, much less serve, this hostile community? Her heart sank as the tall, dark forest began to blot out what little light remained that afternoon. As Joe described life in the mountains, Daisy also realized that this was not a romantic odyssey on which she and Ada had set out. She was beginning to grasp the reality of a great need in this forgotten place. Ada's quivering hand felt Daisy clasp it and squeeze tightly.

"There are three of us," Daisy whispered. "No need to worry." Ada knew she wasn't referring to Joe.

Suddenly, the forest, almost black, was illuminated by a fork of lightning and the darkened sky roared angrily.

"We'd best take shelter at Mabel Selkirk's," Joe muttered, as the crack of his whip echoed along the trail and the plodding nag quickened its pace.

The first warm drops of rain trickled off the girls' bonnets as the wagon climbed the deep-rutted trail and rolled to a stop in front of Mabel Selkirk's humble cabin. Alighting, Ada and Daisy grabbed their suitcases and turned toward the door. Suddenly, Daisy felt Ada's hand on her arm. Ada's breath shortened. She mutely directed her startled companion's eyes towards a huge gnarled tree against which leaned a wild-looking figure. Large, vacant, glazed eyes stared at the newcomers from a tangle of unkempt, shoulder-length hair. His clothes hung in filthy tatters on his ill-fed frame and he moved erratically, shifting nervously from one foot to the other. Daisy sensed almost immediately that he was probably mentally retarded, and she felt strangely frightened by his appearance. He moved clumsily toward the girls and Ada gasped again as, hearing the rattle of a chain, she noticed a heavy fetter about his left ankle, securely anchored to the tree. Daisy's first instinct was horror and extreme revulsion at this spectacle.

Joe's voice broke in cheerfully, "Keeps 'em outa trouble. He's safe thar."

Still shaking, Ada and Daisy turned away to the front of the cabin where Mabel Selkirk waited apprehensively to greet them. Three scantily clad little children clutched her apron, wondering who these strangers could be.

"D'ya mind if we take shelter here till the storm's over?" asked Joe. "This 'ere's Miss Billin's an' Miss Luce, the new missionaries frum th' Bible school."

"Please ta meet ya, jest set a spell an' have a cup o'

buttermilk an' a hot biscuit," she said with timid hospitality. "Oh, Joe, wud ya mind lettin' Horace loose out thar? Bring 'im in out th' rain. He's bin out thar since early mornin'."

Joe left and several moments later re-entered. Horace, lumbering behind, shuffled to a dark corner of the room and collapsed heavily on the rough, wooden floor. Daisy's earlier revulsion melted to compassion for the unfortunate Horace. The single window admitted little light and the air was stale. The crude utensils and dingy atmosphere discouraged the girls' appetites, but not wishing to offend their hostess they downed the buttermilk and biscuits with all the enthusiasm they could muster.

Daisy announced that she and Ada meant to start a Sunday school. She asked Mabel whether she would allow her children to come.

"I s'pose," she said, "can't do 'em no harm, an' I'll git a rest without 'em." Her life was obviously fraught with pain and rugged work. Daisy speculated that she was probably not nearly as old as her appearance suggested.

"Wonderful," Daisy exclaimed. "Only you must promise to send Horace, also." Mabel nodded her agreement, looking at Joe and sharing his surprise.

"Wal, th' storm's over so we best git goin', and thanks fur th' buttermilk, Mabel," said Joe a short while later as he reached for the suitcases and started for the door.

"We are going to have a church service in the schoolhouse on Sunday, Mabel, and we hope you and your husband and family will come," Ada urged.

"I'll try, I dunno 'bout Ben, 'cause he works in th' mine an' I dunno what shift he'll be workin'," she said shyly.

With just a few more miles to go, Joe's old wagon pulled away from the house. A vivid rainbow arched between the mountains was bordering the dusky valley. What a graphic sign God had set before Daisy and Ada on the very first day they entered their first mission field! It reminded them of their covenant-keeping God and renewed their confidence that He would not fail or forsake them.

The road was sloppy after the heavy rain and several times the horse faltered as it struggled to pull the wheels out of the deepening ruts. They arrived at the little cabin that was to be their home just at dusk. Darkness falls fast in the mountains and night there seemed to the girls somehow blacker than it had ever seemed at home. With a cloak of darkness surrounding them, Daisy prayed silently, "Oh, God, make us your lights. Help us to shine in the dark corners of the hearts of these people." Daisy noticed immediately that there were only two small windows—they could not be expected to admit very much light. She remembered the single tiny window in the Selkirks' dreary little cabin.

"How sad, Ada," she remarked. "With such ever changing vistas, you would think these people would have lots of windows."

"Views won't fill yur stomach or keep ya warm," Joe interjected, laying more wood on the fire.

The flames leapt up, licking the cold hearth, bringing warmth and cheer to the drab surroundings, and illuminating the musty interior of the cabin, which Daisy and Ada now examined. Two rusty iron beds sagged deeply under the weight of the lumpy mattresses. The mattresses were tattered and spilling tufts of straw onto the rough-hewn floor, which groaned eerily under every step. A rickety washstand supported an icy porcelain basin and jug, well-worn and badly chipped. Joe carried a burning splinter from the fire to light the two coal-oil lamps which flickered uncertainly at first, then spread their amber glow across the room.

"Well, I must git ta the mine fer my shift," said Joe. "You'll find a few vittels in the kitchen cupboard—'nuf ta git ya started."

Daisy and Ada bade Joe good-night and barred the door. They were exhausted and grateful to be alone at last.

After reading and praying together, Ada extinguished the lamps. Daisy clutched the bedclothes around her and the inky blackness dropped like a velvet cloak on their humble cabin. The journey had been long and arduous and the girls yearned for a sound sleep to refresh them for the commencement of their work on the morrow. As Daisy quickly drifted off to sleep, she was only vaguely aware of the army of lice and ticks that began to stir beneath her, but in any event she was too exhausted to care.

Waking with the first light, she was immediately aware that her skin was frightfully inflamed and ravaged by insect bites. Leaping onto the cold floor she stood aghast at the assembly of insects scurrying purposefully across the sheets.

"Oh, Ada!" she exclaimed, trying to suppress the nausea welling up within her. Ada awoke and on becoming aware of the terrible collection of creatures with which she shared her bed, she instantly joined Daisy on the bare floor where they stood clutching each other and shaking. Daisy's reaction to insect bites and this hostile, strange environment aggravated her usual allergy. Her skin blistered and swelled in unbearable crimson irritation, even as she stood shivering in the early dawn.

"It's the mattresses, Ada. They must go."

Ada, ever sensible, replied, "But, Daisy, what will we sleep on?"

Without responding, Daisy tore off the bedding and dragged her mattress to the back door of the cabin, grabbing a box of matches on the way past the stove. Struggling through the narrow doorway and on into the dusty yard, she turned to see Ada following, her bewildered face—puffed with insect bites—poking out from behind her mattress. Just as Daisy threw her burden down in the dust and struck a match to ignite it, a woman's rasping voice rang out coldly behind her.

"Thars no use in burnin' it, dear; them thar bugs jest come out o' the logs inside. You'd hafta burn down the whole dang cabin an' most of Roarin' Fork to beat them little critters!"

Daisy stood dumbfounded at this advice until the burning match singed her fingers. Then deciding she was beaten, she motioned to the perplexed Ada to return to the cabin with her mattress. Realizing what an extraordinary sight they must have been—disheveled, faces swollen, red-eyed, staggering about in the dewy dawn wearing nothing but night-dresses, lugging old flea-ridden straw mattresses—Daisy succumbed to hilarious laughter.

The unexpected guest helped the girls return their mattresses. Then she stood quietly leaning on a bedstead, breathing heavily from her efforts and the long climb up the hill to the missionaries' cabin. She was perhaps in her fifties, heavy-set and poorly dressed. A discolored bonnet covered all but a fringe of kinky, steel gray hair. At length, she introduced herself as Lucy O'Hara and explained that having heard of their arrival in Roaring Fork, she had struck out early, traveling on foot from her home across the valley to seek help. Her baby grandson had died during the night. A look of utter helplessness on Lucy's face convinced the girls that they must respond.

"You go, Daisy," said Ada. "One of us should stay here in case we are needed, and I can get started cleaning up."

Daisy was not quite sure what help she could bring to Lucy and her family, but she quickly agreed, dressed and, picking up her Bible, joined Lucy for the long walk across the valley.

The sun had climbed above the mountains and now poured its golden life-giving warmth upon the lush countryside. The night rain still gushed down the rutted road, gurgling joyfully like a contented child. The greenery was all slick and glistening. Daisy gazed about her with wide-eyed wonderment, quite forgetting for the moment the sad purpose of her journey. Lucy plodded on ahead, not speaking.

Arriving at her cabin, and easing the door as they entered, Lucy nodded towards her daughter, who sobbed softly on her bed across the dark room.

"Elizabeth, I brung someone. A preacher lady. Sit up."

Her eyes not yet accustomed to the darkness, Daisy approached Elizabeth in gray shadows. Drawing closer she saw a striking young woman pressing the lifeless form of an infant to her tear-stained cheek. "How like an ivory cherub," Daisy thought, her eyes fixed upon the tiny figure with flaxen hair, fine features and perfect little hands and feet! Yet so stiff and icy!

Thrusting the child forward, Elizabeth pleaded, "Dress 'im, please, so Ma kin bury 'im. I jest can't bear ta do it m'self fer I loved 'im so an' now, when we put 'im in the cold earth, I'll never see my darlin' again."

Elizabeth's helplessness struck like cold steel deeply into Daisy's heart. She fought to restrain her own tears, and reached out to take the dead boy from his mother. Lucy pushed some little cotton clothes at her and turning abruptly, left the cabin. Daisy stood frozen for several moments, holding the child and clothes in her outstretched arms, unable to avert her gaze from the terrible sight of her stiff burden. "Here I am," she thought, "my first mission, my first test, and I seem unable to respond." Her heart sank, then she prayed inwardly. "Dear heavenly Father, please do not forsake me here." She laid the infant on the foot of the bed and began to dress him, slowly at first. She managed to put on his booties and began to push his arm into the sleeve of his jacket. The tiny limbs were so stiff and stone cold. When one arm was fitted, Daisy couldn't bear to carry on with the other. She wrapped the jacket around the child's shoulder and held up the dead baby for his mother to see.

"But ya haven't put 'is other arm in!" Elizabeth cried.

Daisy mournfully laid the child down again and finished her work, somewhat ashamed.

She had just completed her morbid task when Lucy returned bearing a small wooden box which she laid down in front of the bed. Looking from Daisy to the baby, she pointed at the box. Daisy laid the baby in the box, but Elizabeth exclaimed, "It's too deep, I can't see 'im!"

The child was taken up again; and after Lucy had stuffed the box with rags and paper, he was lowered once more. Where he rested now, he was clearly visible.

"C'mon," Lucy said. "Wea'l best git on with it." She picked up the box and went out behind the cabin to a grave freshly dug in the soft wet earth.

Daisy helped Elizabeth out of her bed. Having helped the girl put on her shoes, Daisy wrapped a blanket about her and led her to the graveside, Elizabeth muttering throughout, "I'll never see 'im, I'll never see 'im."

Elizabeth wept bitterly as Lucy nailed the cover tight on the box.

"Can ya say a prayer?" Lucy asked, turning to Daisy.

With Elizabeth resting on her arm, Daisy opened her Bible and began to read from John 11:25: "I am the resurrection and the life." She paused from time to time to explain the meaning of what she read, and then continued. She explained that the quality of Christian grief was very different from that of those who sorrow without hope. "Christians can be assured of reuniting with their loved ones who die in Christ before them," she declared. Elizabeth's quivering and sobs were stilled as Daisy spoke. When she had finished, Elizabeth asked Daisy how she could be certain that her own sins were forgiven, and that she would once again hold her infant son. Daisy remembered her grandfather's death and how it had helped to lead her to Jesus. She explained more fully the story of the cross and gently led Elizabeth to its shadow.

Then Lucy lowered the box into the dark hole. Covering it with earth, she took up a stake she had prepared to mark the grave. As she started to thrust it into the sloppy earth, Elizabeth cried, "No! Give me the stake."

Then laying it down on the ground, Elizabeth took another bough and bound it at right angles across the stake. After planting this marker at the head of the little grave she turned and walked bravely back to the cabin.

How different this burial was from that of most inhabitants of this area! Normally the mountain people made a great ceremony of burials, entering into a long time of mourning. They were superstitious, always being sure to lay the departed loved one facing east towards the rising sun. Usually their friends and relatives walked behind the coffin in a long procession to the burial place, and then each one would kiss the face of the departed loved one before they nailed down the lid of the coffin.

Daisy ran breathlessly along the road to her mountain home, where Ada toiled vigorously, wondering what had become of her companion and wishing now she had joined her. Bursting in upon Ada, Daisy joyfully blurted out all that had taken place that morning. Together they offered thanks for the first fruit of their ministry at Roaring Fork.

Daisy and Ada were determined that their rude surroundings would not prevent them from setting a good example for the local residents. They were perpetually scrubbing their cabin, tidying up its shabby furnishings, and tending the neat garden that sprang up around it shortly after their arrival. They received only a token allowance from Nyack and as their work began to fill each day, the girls relied almost totally on neighbors and friends to supply food and basic provisions. As a result, their diet consisted largely of whatever happened to be in surplus supply at the time. Despite their poverty the mountaineers were very generous, often leaving anonymous gifts on the doorstep, too shy to deliver them personally. The girls received more buttermilk than anything else. They drank it, cooked with it, and did just about everything but wash in it. Yet they were receiving far more than they could possibly consume. When Daisy determined to return the excess, Elizabeth advised her that such action would be interpreted by the mountain people as ingratitude. Faced with an ever increasing supply of buttermilk, Ada began to distribute it to the schoolchildren who flocked to the tumble-down schoolhouse nearby, and in the end, Daisy went so far as to dig a hole by night and pour in jugs of turning buttermilk.

Before very long the schoolhouse, which had sat idle the previous winter waiting for a teacher, once more echoed with the ring of childish voices. Ada taught while Daisy visited as many homes as she could reach, sealing friendships with the stoic mountain women and opening the Scriptures to their hungry hearts. What joy she felt to see these women arriving with their children for services at the little schoolhouse on Sunday mornings.

Of course, Daisy's visits were not all pleasant. Often she was very rudely received and sometimes taunted by local hoodlums who lurked along her way. Tragedy struck the mountain people with cruel regularity. Mine shafts collapsing left bitter orphans. Fever gripped the old, weak and very young. The frightful specter of Horace and others like him, caged or shackled, confronted Daisy again and again as she traveled about the valley. And as the confidence of the mountaineers in Daisy and Ada grew steadily, the weeks stretching to months, they came to rely upon the girls for medical and dental treatment as well as burial of their dead.

It was a steaming August Sunday morning. Daisy and Ada had been two months in the mountains. Waking very early, they prayed about the morning service as the sun peeked above the mountain. While Daisy reviewed the notes of the sermon she had prepared, Ada went cheerily about fixing breakfast. Through the tiny window Daisy gazed silently down the sleeping valley.

"Our work is going quite well here, Ada. The women and the children seem to respond. But the men don't seem to care much."

"They're a rather rough lot," Ada replied.

"I went down to the mine yesterday," Daisy continued, "and invited Joe to come this morning. But he only laughed."

As she finished speaking, the sound of wagons drawing up across the road at the schoolhouse interrupted the conversation and the girls gathered their Bibles and hurried across to start the service.

Entering from the back, they stopped short and stared at the congregation in amazement. The handful of faithful women had been joined by a large group of dusty coal miners. They were wearing the same tattered, soot-covered overalls they wore down in the mine. Some were mere boys, others gruff old fellows whose deep-lined faces belied their true ages. Almost to a man they chewed on great slimy wads of tobacco, pausing now and then to roll them about their mouths. Obviously the women were delighted at the presence of their menfolk. And sitting boldly in the front row, grinning broadly, was Joe.

"I brung sum o' ma friends, Miss Billin's," he quipped, gesturing toward the overflowing crowd.

Hymn books, quickly dispersed, ran short. But as most present were illiterate, it made little difference. While Ada took her place at the pump organ, Daisy announced a familiar hymn and then pumped furiously so the melody could be heard over the lusty voices of the miners.

Later, Daisy rose from her upturned ash can to deliver the morning sermon. She tried to ignore the many disturbances which had become commonplace to her by now. Her earnest remarks were occasionally punctuated by the disagreeable sound of tobacco juice spewed across the crowded room to spread in splatters on a wall, or by the abrupt snort of one of the great filthy hogs that so often took an active part in the services, wandering aimlessly down the aisle or across the platform. Sometimes a drunkard, forgetting for the moment where he was, would begin to sing as he staggered about. Despite all of this, Daisy had always found that most of the mountain folk treated her and Ada with great respect and she never really feared them, for all their rough ways.

Joe had listened attentively. After the service closed and Daisy and Ada had greeted each member of the congregation, they turned to find Joe still in his seat. In the following few moments the girls were able to lead him to Christ.

After that Joe became a great help. The neglected schoolhouse began to receive attention and long overdue repairs got underway. Many of the miners continued to attend services on Sunday morning, often at Joe's insistence. He destroyed his still and soon was coming by often to learn to read so that he could begin to study the Bible on his own.

By early fall the diet of buttermilk and biscuits and the endless battle against insect bites, rashes and hives were beginning to have their effect. Daisy's weight was down to about eighty pounds, her face thin and her eyes hollowing. Ada too was not well. One September morning Joe arrived at their cabin, as he so often did, with a sharp knock at the door.

"Wud ya be wishin' to go ketch some fish down at the river?" he asked as Daisy opened the door.

"Fish for dinner! What a lovely change, Joe!" Daisy replied.

In all her childhood years in Peterborough, so conveniently surrounded by many lakes, each teeming with fish, Daisy had never tried to catch any of them. She eagerly agreed to Joe's suggestion and, together with Ada, followed him down to where the cool mountain river gushed through the valley, gathering here and there in small pools before continuing its headlong dash from the hills. Joe had made up extra lines for the girls and while they winced, he baited their hooks, explaining, as he worked, the best technique for fishing.

Daisy and Ada tossed their lines into the river and settled down on the bank to enjoy the warmth of the rising sun. Suddenly, Ada lurched toward the river, her pole flexing erratically as she struggled to her feet; she called helplessly to Joe. Almost immediately Daisy's pole arched violently towards the water until a full one-third of it disappeared below the surface. With both girls crying out in excitement and struggling with their straining poles, lines became hopelessly entangled as the big mountaineer waded to his waist in the river, finally gathering two fiercely fighting fish into his old net.

"Well done, ladies! Well done!" he exclaimed as both girls fell back on the bank in exhausted disbelief.

All morning they fished with great success. They climbed the road once more to their cabin, Joe hauling the fish.

"You certainly know how to catch fish, Joe," remarked Daisy. "Did you know that Jesus' first followers were poor fishermen? He found them mending nets by the seashore and called them to be fishers of men. They obeyed Him and today their 'catch' is spread throughout the world."

"D'ya think Jesus cud make a poor fellar like me a fisher of men?" Joe asked cautiously.

"Joe," Daisy said, stooping to face him, "what would have happened today if Ada and I had decided to go fishing without you, if we prepared our own equipment, searched out our own fishing hole, chosen our bait, baited our hooks and fished our own way?"

Joe laughed heartily. "Ya wudda caught nuthin', 'cept maybe an ol' boot!"

"That's right," continued Daisy, "but although we had to do our part, we followed your direction and learned from your words and example, and just look at the result! Jesus will surely make you a fisher of men for Him if you obey Him and follow wherever He leads you."

They arrived at the cabin and parted, Joe hurrying off down the mountain again for his shift at the mine. That night the girls dined on fresh fish and in all the years since, fish never tasted as good to them as on that occasion. Some summers later Daisy would see her own two sons returning with a fine catch of fish, and the sight would bring Joe back to her mind. She would recall how he had hungered for spiritual food in the autumn of 1911 along that dusty mountain road winding up to her cabin in West Virginia. She discovered later that Joe had begun to travel about Appalachia on foot, preaching wherever listeners would gather, and that his catch for Jesus was very great indeed! For Daisy, Joe was the seed that fell on good ground and flourished long after she had moved on.

Ada dropped her fork and sighed heavily.

"I simply can't eat another morsel of fish, Daisy!"

A rapping at the door sent Ada scurrying to open it. The station master at Roaring Fork stood quietly on the porch, looking very grave. He fumbled in his waistcoat pocket and thrust forward a special delivery letter. Ada took it, and saying good-night closed the door.

Daisy sensed as Ada opened the letter that a chapter in her life was about to close abruptly. As two one-way tickets fluttered to the floor, she was not surprised to learn that Ada's mother was dying in Toronto and Ada was wanted home immediately. There was no discussion on the point. Daisy somehow knew that her time among her mountain friends was almost over and she too must go with Ada, who had refused to let Daisy come alone to Roaring Fork months before.

Several days later the two girls stood at the back of the caboose as it began to pull slowly away from Roaring Fork. The platform was crowded with their congregation.

Amid the cluster of mountaineers Daisy recognized some of her own dresses and articles of clothing, which she had dispersed to some of the women. Many wept. When the train reached the end of the platform, Joe struck up a hymn and the two young missionaries could still hear their singing echo down the valley long after the little group of their mountain flock had faded from view.

4

Daisy the Deaconess

They buried Mrs. Luce on a chill November afternoon. The tailored black coats, somber silk hats, and
well-ordered funeral procession through post-Edwardian
Toronto contrasted sharply with the rude disorder of West
Virginia burials which Daisy had attended all too frequently during the preceding months. Mr. Luce struck Daisy as a
particularly pitiful figure. He was in his late fifties, quite
gray, but robust and energetic. His family had been his
greatest joy. He would have given all his possessions to
preserve it. But now his dear wife was taken—the very
one for whom he cared most. Daisy shared his grief as she
watched him, bareheaded, sobbing bitterly at the graveside, his great cloak encircling Ada and her young brother.

Ada's home seemed very empty in the days that followed. Mr. Luce begged Daisy to stay on in his home to
comfort his mourning daughter.

Although Daisy dearly wished to turn her hand
again to Christian work, she felt that her debt to Ada and
her family was very great, and of course she had
exhausted all her financial resources. Recognizing that

God wanted her to pause awhile and await His voice, Daisy agreed to stay in the Luce household, on condition that she be permitted to take over domestic chores until Ada's father had been repaid the train fare from Roaring Fork. Mr. Luce was delighted with Daisy's decision and in his generous way agreed reluctantly to her condition.

This began one of the mysterious waiting periods in Daisy's life. She was to experience a great many more in the years ahead. These twilights of Christian experience were most perplexing. Some years later in life Daisy discovered that many in service for God faced this phenomenon—missionary candidates were plagued by interminable delays, red tape, lack of financial support, medical missionaries anxiously awaited essential supplies, graduates of Bible schools, Christian colleges and universities impatiently longed for a call—all had a feeling of total preparedness yet lacked a place to serve. She decided that it is perhaps a simple test of patience or of willingness to accept the wisdom of God, which goes far beyond human comprehension. Or maybe it is not a test at all; one may be totally prepared for the task he covets, but not in the least ready for the work God has for him. Whatever the reason, it can be a most perplexing time. Ultimately Daisy found that frustration gives way to fulfillment, confusion yields to comfort, restlessness turns to reward. She did not always see the ground over which she walked, but ever tried to keep her eyes on higher ground.

Early in 1911, Daisy persuaded her family to move to Toronto from Peterborough. After she had spent three months in Ada's home, the Billings family was reunited and settled in a little home at 611 Euclid Avenue. Daisy enrolled in the deaconess training course conducted under the auspices of the mission board of the Presbyterian Church in Canada. Her decision came after much prayer and frequent discussions with Ada. The course was thorough and intensive although brief.

Graduation brought a very modest, but adequate stipend and the strange new world of working under close direction and supervision of the Presbyterian Church. This was quite unlike her service at Roaring Fork, and demanded a dramatic adjustment.

Daisy's first task was to prepare a book regarding the history of the deaconess movement in the Presbyterian Church. Her temperament was activist and something as academic as the writing of history seemed to Daisy wasteful of her energies. To make matters worse, she quickly discovered that her knowledge of the subject was at best superficial. Yet Daisy was determined to carry out the job and attacked it zestfully, reading all she could, interviewing everyone who knew anything about the subject and finally drafting, and redrafting, her manuscript. In time, the Presbyterians realized that this slight young woman, raised in the Christian and Missionary Alliance Church, had become something of an expert on this aspect of Presbyterian history. She was invited to speak on the subject to large enthusiastic gatherings, and it was in these meetings that Daisy began to recognize her penchant for public speaking, and to sharpen her skill in this area.

She spent many hours preparing her addresses, often writing out every word in longhand. Yet when she stepped upon a platform before a crowd, she exuded spontaneity. Small of stature, dressed in her prim uniform complete with bonnet, she seemed unassuming enough, but her voice had a quality which was most unusual. Her approach was earnest and directly personal, giving the unique impression to her listeners that this diminutive figure had come to speak only to them, that she had something momentous to say, and that she particularly wanted to say it to them. One of Daisy's most endearing qualities was the abrupt and unexpected humor with which she punctuated her addresses, turning somber faces instantly to laughter and then with swift and sudden precision striking soberly to the heart of the matter. The importance of those early speaking engagements was that God gave to her a recognition of her preaching gift. Until then she had not suspected that she could communicate effectively to large crowds of people. Yet it seemed the larger the crowd the more potent her preaching. God had used the apparently dreary task of writing the history of the deaconess movement in the Presbyterian Church to reveal a latent gift.

Daisy's ability to preach and evoke a positive response from her listeners did not long escape the attention of Rev. J. D. Morrow. He was one of the most colorful men of pre-World War I Toronto, and almost certainly the most bombastic clergyman. His preaching was renowned and could only be described as electrifying and eccentric. It was, of course, very effective. A unique clergyman, Morrow had an irresistible personality. He was pastor of Dale Presbyterian Church in Toronto in the summer of 1912. His congregation met in the basement of a partially completed structure. This devout and incredibly energetic pastor was indeed a celebrated character. He decided not to wear a hat until the roof was on his church. He went about Toronto on a motorcycle with Daisy seated behind him. His locks flowed freely under a canopy which covered the vehicle and often protected them from torrential downpours. All of these unique features only added to the natural dignity of the man. He was greatly loved by all who knew him.

Mr. Morrow invited Daisy to join him at Dale and she eagerly accepted. She had tired of recounting the history of the deaconess movement, and was determined to *make* some of it instead. This was the chance for which she had waited. Surely this was a call to her life's work, the beginning of a long and vibrant ministry. She told her mother that at last God had placed her in the front lines— permanently. Of this fact she was certain.

Daisy took up her duties as deaconess at Dale as the spring of 1914 turned to summer. Her activities were extremely varied and kept her busy indeed. First, there was the need of her own congregation, which was beginning to grow very rapidly under Pastor Morrow's flamboyant and dynamic leadership. He could not possibly carry on all his pastoral duties alone. Much of the visitation of the sick and invalid members of the congregation fell to Daisy, as did the personal counseling. As the membership roll grew ever larger, the demands on the little deaconess multiplied. It was through this contact with her own congregation that Daisy began to realize that there were vast numbers of people in the very shadow of the church who were in desperate physical and spiritual need. As she went about the city on visitation she concluded that she could not continue to pass by the stricken poor of Toronto and determined to expand her ministry.

She turned first to the stream of immigrants gravitating to Toronto from every part of Europe in search of work. Often they had no friends or family in Canada and struggled with the English language. Loneliness and alienation stalked them relentlessly. Daisy began by organizing welcoming parties and assisting newcomers to find friendship, a spiritual home and employment.

Her work in the slums began the following winter. It was arduous and committed volunteers and helpers were scarce. Daisy often found herself alone as she brought comfort and what food she could assemble to those in extreme and abject circumstances. Although this work continued almost unnoticed year round, it was warmly commended and heartily supported at Christmas time, when Daisy administered the "Santa Claus Fund" with the cooperation of a local daily paper. Donations solicited through the press were applied towards food and clothing which were distributed to those on her growing list of poor and needy.

Daisy's work frequently took her to many parts of the city and before long she became a welcome sight to eyes hollowed with hunger, vacant with loneliness and despair, or tired as a result of long suffering. At just five feet, her prim uniform always neatly pressed, bonnet carefully set, she was known by many as the "Little Lady," not least of all by the streetcar drivers who, recognizing her between their stops, would gladly wait to pick her up, thus shortening her journey and lightening her load.

Four new deaconesses went into this ministry as it flourished under Daisy's guidance. This was a great joy to her, as were the teaching and prayer ministries which she pursued vigorously. But perhaps her greatest delight was taken in the fact that her pastor allowed her to preach once each month to his congregation, for she loved to preach.

At first she worried that a membership which had grown accustomed to the colorful and unpredictable preaching of this rare man of God would have difficulty accepting hers. But Daisy had underestimated her own appeal. The people responded in tears and laughter, in thanksgiving and service. These months of regular preaching left little doubt in her mind—preaching was her forte. Though physically diminutive, the great strength of her spirit and sincerity of her faith emerged to fill the largest auditorium. She combined this natural gift with hard preparatory effort, studying, praying, drafting and redrafting her sermons.

No one appreciated Daisy's preaching more than Mr. Morrow himself. "Make them cry, Miss Billings, they love to cry!" he would counsel. Of course, Daisy knew that he meant that the children of God longed to hear a message from their heavenly Father. It moved them deeply. Often this senior pastor was so touched by her sermons that he would break into a hymn before she had finished; the congregation would join him and sing it through meaningfully before Daisy could continue.

In the spring of 1916, the main sanctuary of Dale was completed. One Sunday morning in April J. D. Morrow announced to the congregation that the following Sunday evening would witness the last service to be held in the church basement. It was symbolic in a way that, after their long and sacrificial faithfulness, these dear people would be moving up into their beautiful new sanctuary where they could worship God without the distraction and dislocation of the building program. "Miss Daisy Billings will preach the final sermon in the basement of the church," Mr. Morrow announced. Daisy was thunderstruck! She had never expected such an honor, and had no warning that this well-known Toronto preacher would graciously give her this priceless privilege.

Daisy spent the next week in prayer and meditation. God gave her a stirring message which she delivered in her inimitable style on the great occasion. She concluded by challenging her listeners. This could not mark the end of their dedication and sacrifice, she declared. They must not relax and bask in the comfort of their new building. It was an instrument, a tool which God had given them, and they must turn it to His advantage, to His glory. Without this continued devotion and service, all that they had worked towards would count as nothing. Again they wept and resolved to meet the challenge. At the conclusion of the service, Daisy was more convinced than ever that this was where she belonged. At last God had demonstrated the power of the gift he had bestowed on her. She was to be a preacher.

Several days later, while still riding the crest of this peak in her ministry, Daisy was called to the pastor's office. He seemed nervous and uncertain. He began timidly.

"Miss Billings, the membership has grown rapidly in recent months. It's a very great responsibility for us."

"I know," responded Daisy. "But God will give us what we need to do the job."

Mr. Morrow smiled. "Exactly, and I think the time has come when we need a full-fledged assistant minister to help me. This will enable you to give all your energies to the work of a deaconess. I have found a young man whom I believe to be suitable. His name is Oswald Smith."

Daisy was crestfallen and fought to contain the bitter disappointment welling up within her. "Oh, no, sir. That would in my opinion be most unwise. It might be difficult for a new person to fit in and gain the confidence of the people. In any case, it would be risky indeed to accept a full-time assistant until he has proven himself. Perhaps we could give him a few minor tasks until he can be properly evaluated. He may fall flat on his face!"

The pastor listened patiently. He knew Daisy loved her work and was now jealously guarding it. When she had finished he responded, "Well, Miss Billings, I'm not very often wrong on things like this. I certainly wasn't wrong about you, was I?"

Daisy blushed. She knew the decision had been made and nothing she could say would reverse it. Sadly she left his office; she was confused and slightly bitter. Why had God brought her this far, only to set her aside and give the work that satisfied her most to some untried, unknown fellow? It was clear to her that she could not possibly compete with a man. The bitterness clung to her for several days until Mr. Morrow invited her to come to his home one evening for dinner to meet Oswald Smith. At first she most instinctively wanted to decline, but realized that she should go. Perhaps she could yet demonstrate to her determined pastor that hiring this inexperienced young usurper was a mistake.

"By the way, Miss Billings," said Mr. Morrow, "this is a social occasion and you should wear a pretty dress. We see enough of your uniform throughout the week."

When the fateful evening arrived, in a fit of stubbornness, Daisy methodically put on her deaconess' uniform, adjusted her bonnet and set out on the streetcar for Mr. Morrow's home.

She alighted just one block from her destination and

immediately noticed a very tall, thin, fair young man stepping from the streetcar across the road. They both started on opposite sides of the street for Mr. Morrow's and Daisy concluded that this must be Oswald Smith.

As they reached the Morrows' home together they mounted the front steps and rang the bell. The young man spoke, "You must be Miss Billings, the deaconess," he said. "I am Mr. Smith."

Daisy was about to speak when Mr. Morrow opened the door and exclaimed, "Well, I didn't know you two were acquainted. I see you are starting out together. Let's hope you end together," he said jokingly.

Later that evening Mr. Morrow cautioned that they must never be seen together except on church business. They were to address each other as "Mr. Smith" and "Miss Billings." All of this seemed most unnecessary as far as Daisy was concerned and she protested politely that she for one would have no difficulty heeding his admonitions. Oswald made no reply although Daisy thought she saw his lively blue eyes twinkle, as though he were contemplating all the church business which might want discussion.

Daisy was not far wrong. Over the six months following, Oswald never lost an opportunity to discuss church business with Daisy. These were their only contacts apart from funerals, when they were expected to ride together to the graveside; but, of course, such occasions offered little opportunity for socializing.

If Daisy had been able to peek at Oswald's diary during those days, she would have been surprised to read these words in May 1916: "Daisy is one of the most beautiful characters I have ever met. Her spiritual life is very deep and earnest. She has a beautiful sympathetic nature and is refined in every way. During the last few months my affection has continued to grow and now I know she is God's choice for me."

In June 1916, he wrote, "Precious girl! She is more to me than she will ever know, and far far sweeter than I ever dreamed."

Despite the fact that Oswald constantly found it necessary to discuss church business with her, Daisy ultimately concluded with relief that his interest in her was after all only professional. This conclusion was arrived at after she became aware that Oswald was corresponding with a girl in Chicago, where he had gone to school.

During one of the visits of this girl to Toronto, Oswald unexpectedly invited Daisy to join him one afternoon to examine a house he was contemplating purchasing. At first, Daisy couldn't understand why he didn't take his girl friend along, but decided that he was planning to surprise her, and wanted a feminine opinion before buying. On that basis Daisy decided to go.

The house was on Garden Avenue in Toronto, in a neat but modest neighborhood. Number 57 was indeed charming. Oswald rang the bell; a matronly lady opened the door and exclaimed, "Oh, and this must be Mrs. Smith!"

Daisy couldn't hide her embarrassment, and as Oswald grinned mischievously, Daisy stammered, "Definitely not! I'm Miss Billings, a deaconess at Mr. Smith's church. He just wanted my opinion on this house."

A little confused by Daisy's barbed reply, the lady proceeded to show them through the house. Oswald made doubly sure that Daisy saw every closet and cupboard. When they stood on the street outside once more, he asked, "Well, Miss Billings, what do you think of it?"

"It's a very pleasant, comfortable house, Mr. Smith. I have no doubt you will make someone very happy here," Daisy replied.

Later that evening the doorbell at the Billings home rang. "Oh, bother," sighed Daisy, "another of Mr. Smith's business calls. He certainly has a great deal of church business to discuss," she thought, as she opened the door. To her great surprise and shock, a bouquet of roses was thrust toward her and behind them stood a beaming Oswald Smith. Daisy was completely flustered. The flowers were totally unexpected. Clumsily she showed Oswald to the parlor, then disappeared to the kitchen to get a vase and collect her thoughts. Returning to the parlor, she found Oswald seated by the window, nervously adjusting his collar. He was handsome against the light; his strong facial features were well defined and his piercing blue eyes and blond hair gave him a look of distinction.

"What business could he be about tonight?" Daisy wondered. She was still bewildered. "What about the girl from Chicago? Could I have been wrong about her? Then there's the house—what about that?" These questions raced through her mind.

Oswald looked up as Daisy entered and began to arrange the flowers, turning her back to him. "Miss Billings, will you go for a drive with me tomorrow to Mr. Morrow's summer cottage? I've cleared it with him."

Before she knew what she was saying, Daisy agreed to go. They briefly discussed some church matters and Oswald left abruptly, hurrying with great long strides down the street to catch a streetcar. Daisy was left contemplating the roses.

"He must have something very serious, even personal, to discuss with me," she thought. Systematically she began to consider the possibilities, and was able to eliminate all but one. It struck her like a lightning bolt. "What if he has really fallen in love with me and wants to marry me? What could I possibly say?" she wondered. "Do I really want to get married?" No married woman went on with her work in those days, and Daisy's work was her life. She had spent years training for it and she felt so fulfilled and happy doing what she felt God had called her to do. She did not need a man. She was happy the way she was. She could preach, and was as much a leader as he was. Could she ever be satisfied to stay in a house and take care of a husband and family? Daisy looked at the big clock ticking away on the wall and realized she was already late for an appointment to visit a member of the church who was ill at home. She took a look at herself in the mirror, planted her deaconess' bonnet firmly on her head, tied the ribbon of it under her chin and, taking one final look at herself, said aloud with determination, I am *bound to be free!"*

Down the street Daisy trotted at top speed, pushing all the silly thoughts she had been thinking out of her mind until she arrived at her destination. She felt a little preoccupied all the time she was talking to the patient. After she had prayed with her and tried to encourage her, Daisy started for home.

Although exhausted emotionally and physically, she could not get to sleep that night. She kept tossing over in her mind the events of the day and, closeted in the privacy of her thoughts, she began thinking about the fact that she had told Mr. Smith she would go to Mr. Morrow's cottage the next day with him alone. Again she listed the many sound reasons for not encouraging Oswald Smith.

She had just reached the peak of her ministry. If she kept on, she might even get to other countries to preach. "How I would love to visit foreign countries," she thought. "It will be all up with me now if I marry him. I'll never get anywhere! Besides, the Presbyterian Mission Board is paying me twelve hundred dollars as assistant at the church. How could two of us live on his salary, half the salary I am getting now? I don't want to be bound by the chains of home and husband. What a night this is turning out to be! I might as well get up. I can't sleep," she concluded as she threw back the covers.

She climbed out of bed, walked over to the window in the silence of the night and looked out at the brilliance of the stars shining in the inky, black sky. "Maybe I am being presumptuous. Maybe he won't ask me, and I have lost all this sleep for nothing. But why does this cause such a conflict within me? Why can't I just say No once and for all to him? There are a few things about him that I don't even like, but then I suppose I could fix them after I married him as far as that goes. He is a good preacher, and he writes beautiful hymns and poetry. I think he has some potential, but then so have I."

"Oh, well," she sighed sleepily, "I'll have to keep my promise and go with him tomorrow, and I'll have to let him know just how I feel. I hope he won't bring up the subject," she said aloud as she climbed back into bed and tried to catch a little sleep before it was time to get up.

5

Only a Ring

When Daisy went down for breakfast, her sister Ruth had already left for work. Daisy was sorry she did not see Ruth before she left because she wanted to talk to someone. "I'll phone her," Daisy thought. Ruth answered the phone.

"What is wrong, Daisy? Why are you calling me at work so early in the morning? Has anything happened?"

"Quite a lot has happened, Ruth, and I don't know yet if it is wrong or right," Daisy replied.

"Well go ahead, tell me. What is it?"

"I am going to tell you something, Ruth," Daisy said, "and I don't want you to tell anyone unless I prove to be right. Ever since I learned that Mr. Morrow was inviting that new minister, Mr. Smith, to assist him at the church I've had a presentiment that I was going to marry him. He has asked me to go to Mr. Morrow's cottage with him today alone, and my presentiment is growing ever stronger. Don't you tell anyone, Ruth, because I could be wrong."

"All right, Daisy. You probably are wrong. I can't

imagine you marrying anyone. You never have been interested in marriage. Your work is everything. It sure will surprise me if that happens. I will be anxious to hear how you got along when I get home tonight."

Mr. Smith, always punctual, had said he would meet Daisy at two o'clock, and he arrived right on the dot of two. It was a warm, sunny day in May 1916. Spring flowers were coming into bloom in all the gardens along the way to the Morrows' cottage on the lake in Mimico near Toronto. The woods were alive with the singing of the birds and trilliums were in abundance on every side. As they approached the cottage they could hear the splashing of the waves on the rocky coastline. All nature was vibrant and happy with the arrival of spring.

Oswald and Daisy walked along the shore, drinking in the beauty of the surroundings and listening to the perfect rhythm of the waves. "Only God could create little birds to sing such beautiful songs every spring, could bring from tiny buds such fragrant blossoms," Daisy pondered. 'Only God could by the pressure of His almighty hand cause the waves to roll and crash in such sparkling beauty." Something awakened her whole being with the arrival of spring. The sky was bluer and the soft white clouds more fleecy and more beautiful than ever before. Daisy was so glad to be alive and a part of the surrounding beauty and joy of spring. "What is it?" she wondered. "Why do I feel so unusually happy? Could it be that I am in love?"

Oswald suggested they sit on a big log by the water to watch the waves, and chat for a while. He talked about many things, discussing their varied backgrounds, families, goals, dreams and aspirations. Daisy sensed that he was leading up to something and, sure enough, she was right.

"Miss Billings," said Oswald, getting right to the point. "I love you very much, and I want you to be my wife. Will you?"

Daisy was speechless. She knew now that she loved him and she felt a prisoner of his love, a prisoner that had no desire to escape. He had captured her heart in spite of her will to be free.

"Yes, Mr. Smith, I love you too. I want to be your wife," she responded timidly, hardly able to believe it was she, Miss Billings, the ambitious deaconess, agreeing to be married. Was she really willing to yield her freedom to become the wife of this young minister? She remembered how she had tried to discourage Mr. Morrow from bringing Oswald to the church as an assistant. Yet now she had consented to marry him! Daisy once thought she knew God's plan for her life. How wrong she was!

The phone rang directly after supper the next night. "Miss Billings," said the excited voice on the other end. "It's a beautiful evening, and I wonder if you would like to go canoeing with me on the Humber River? I could call for you in about an hour. Would that be all right?"

Daisy had not been canoeing since her Peterborough childhood. "Oh, yes, Mr. Smith, I will be ready," she replied eagerly.

The river was very calm. Only the gentle dip of the paddle disturbed the stillness of the beautiful Humber that evening. After they had glided along the shore, mutely absorbing the glorious colors of the fading sunset, Oswald stopped paddling and steadied the canoe in a little cove. From his pocket he pulled a tiny box, and said, "I have something for you." Opening the box, he took out a sparkling little diamond ring and placed it on Daisy's finger. "I want to seal our engagement tonight with this ring!" he said. "It is only a ring, but it means that I love you." In awesome silence Daisy stared at the glistening jewel.

"Well," Oswald continued, "are you going to kiss me?" Daisy, feeling that she was having a beautiful dream, kissed him tenderly. As she did, Oswald reached for a scrap of paper on which he had scrawled some words and began to read:

'Twas only a ring that I gave you, dear,
   Neath the light of the stars above,
And oh, it seemed such a little thing,
   But it sealed, it sealed our love;
Then wear it, dear, while the years go by,
   My own true love forever;
And from that hour that made us one
   May naught arise to sever.

'Twas only a ring, yes, only a ring
   That I placed upon your hand,
But let us not think of the value, dear,
   If our hearts would understand.
For it takes us back to the hallowed spot
   Where first we told the story.
And it bears us on to the coming years,
   The promise of love's glory.

'Twas only a ring, but it told you, dear,
   Of a love that would not die.
Away in the woods by the riverside,
   And under the starlit sky;

With never a sound but the paddle dip,
  And the murmur of voices low
Or the tender strains of a plaintive song
  As the boats passed to and fro.

'Twas only a ring, but the night throbbed on,
  And it seemed so hard to part,
For the mystic spell of a joy unknown
  Had stolen upon your heart.
Then wear it, dear, while the years go by,
  My own true love forever;
And from that hour that made us one
  May naught arise to sever!

(From *Poems of a Lifetime*, p. 64)

Daisy soon discovered that Oswald had the romantic heart of a poet. This was the first of many beautiful poems which she inspired him to write. Other poems he wrote for her were entitled "Together," "The Betrothal" and "My Darling," all of which were published years later in his book, *Poems of a Lifetime.*

After a rather short engagement they were married on September 12, 1916, in Dale Presbyterian Church. It was a modest wedding. Daisy's mother made her wedding suit in white trimmed with blue. It was not the custom to give bridal showers in those days. The only wedding gifts received were from various organizations of the church. The Sunday school gave them a cut glass fruit bowl with eight matching fruit dishes. Daisy treasured it because the Sunday school meant so much to her.

Oswald was kept waiting for half an hour at the church. Taxis were in short supply during wartime. The one Daisy ordered to pick her up went to the wrong address. However, there was nothing Oswald could do but patiently pace up and down, looking anxiously out the window. Rev. J. D. Morrow and John McNichol, the principal of Toronto Bible College, officiated at the ceremony.

Daisy had not expected the enormous crowd that packed the church and pressed around the outside trying to get in. It consisted mostly of recent immigrants and the poor whom she had frequently visited as a deaconess. It was necessary for the police to make a way for her to get into the church as the crowds thronged the streets. The occasion resembled a funeral more than a wedding. All the people whom Daisy had come to know and to love wept bitterly. They knew that this marked the end of her deaconess work, including visits to them in their homes. Very few, if any, women worked after their marriage. They thought they would never see Daisy again, and for the most part they were correct. At the end of the ceremony, much to Daisy's surprise, Mr. Morrow leaned forward and said, as he kissed his little deaconess, "I have waited a long time to do this." As she emerged from the church afterwards the onlookers showered the beaming couple with rice. A grain lodged in Daisy's eye and she did not see much of what happened after that.

The next day the newspapers highlighted the event with photos of the bride and groom.

Oswald's father was a telegraph operator for the Canadian Pacific Railway and he gave them a pass to go by train to see Ottawa, Hull and Quebec City. They had very little money and Oswald had to borrow fifty dollars for the honeymoon. Later he paid it back with interest.

They had never been on a vacation anywhere, and they wanted to do as much sightseeing as possible. Their only transportation for their three days in the city was by

ASSISTANT PASTOR OF NEW DALE PRESBYTERIAN CHURCH WEDS ITS POPULAR DEACONESS.

Rev. Oswald Smith and Deaconess Billings, whom he wedded last night at the church where they were co-laborers.

Seldom has Toronto seen a larger wedding than that last evening when about two thousand people crowded the new Dale Presbyterian Church to witness the marriage of its beloved deaconess, Miss Daisy Billings, second daughter of Mr. and Mrs George Billings, Dufferin street, to Rev. Oswald J. Smith, the assistant pastor of the church, and son of Mr. and Mrs. B. Smith. Rev. J. D. Morrow, assisted by Rev. J. McNicol, performed the ceremony, which took place on the pulpit platform. The bride was prettily attired in a cream serge suit with blue silk trimmings and hat to match and wore a corsage bouquet of roses. The bride entered the church on the arm of her father to the strains of the wedding march played by Miss Lorna Hughes. During the signing of the register Mr. McBretney sang "All Joy be Thine." Messrs. John Porter and Fred Rutherford were ushers, Mr. and Mrs. Smith later left directly for Quebec and other eastern points and on their return will reside at 58 Garden avenue.

The newspaper account of the wedding of Oswald and Daisy.

foot. They could not afford to stay in hotels, and so spent the nights with Oswald's relatives.

The highlight of their honeymoon, however, was their visit to the cathedral of Ste. Anne de Beaupré. They found out, to their dismay, that there was a charge to tour through it. Seated on a bench in front of the cathedral Oswald turned to Daisy and said, "You definitely should see this, Daisy, but I have enough money for only one of us to go, so I'll stay here on this bench while you make the tour."

"I would love to see it," answered Daisy, "but I think you should go and I'll wait here for you." Daisy was glad for the chance to rest her tired little feet—they had been fairly running to keep up with Oswald's big strides while sightseeing all day.

Oswald returned from his tour just in time to board the train for home. His aunt had packed them a lunch to eat on the train. Tired but happy, they arrived at their home on Garden Avenue in Toronto. They called it Garden Rest. They were so tired when they reached home after tramping the streets of Quebec that they thought this would be an appropriate name for their new home.

Daisy now had to get adjusted to her role in life as a minister's wife. Withdrawing from the public life she had been used to, no longer active as a deaconess, she now took her place beside her husband, sharing the burden of the work to which he was called. For her a new "pulpit" was erected, a new witness stand from which some of the sweetest and most helpful ministries of Christian grace and blessing were still to come.

Daisy became quite domesticated and enjoyed fixing up their home to make it inviting and cozy. She delighted in matching colors as much as possible on her limited allowance, in making her curtains and most of her clothes. On June 21, 1916, Oswald wrote in his diary, "It has been a great joy to fix up our home and I am finding 'my darling' more and more precious every day. What a wealth of love and affection she has! It's like a man looking for gold dust and finding a nugget. How good God has been to me! Little do I deserve it all! She has worked her own way through life with little assistance. Oh, how I want to love her with all my heart next to Him, and make her happy." Daisy always felt a minister's wife should look as well-groomed and attractive as possible—if people in other walks of life thought it necessary to look their best for the work they represented, how much more should Christians look their best for the Lord, the One whom they represented!

Though Oswald and Daisy had come from different backgrounds and had many varied interests, one goal was common to both of them, and that was the spreading of the gospel to every creature. This was their greatest and deepest burning desire and purpose for living. This they shared throughout life. As they journeyed along the unknown pathway, they proved that no life could be happier or more rewarding, in spite of the many valleys they had to traverse to reach the mountain peaks.

6

Role Changes

They called it the Great War. It had begun in a flush of imperial fervor in 1914 and would draw aimlessly to its tragic conclusion four years later. It was the first of two world-wide armed cataclysms which would dismantle the British Empire and shape the modern world. It was the first real indication that henceforward men would indeed live in a global village. As the conflict plodded on, first into months, then years, the network of bloodstained trenches scarring the groaning bulk of Western Europe grew ever larger. The call went out to members of the British Commonwealth for more recruits, more "cannon fodder." The cream of Canadian youth answered the call and joined one of the festive parades along King Street in Toronto, with bands and pipers and cheering crowds of old men, young children and women. If these eager new recruits knew that this parade along King Street emptied into dank and deathly trenches somewhere in France, already rank with the rotting flesh of those who had gone before, nothing in their beaming, prideful faces belied it. Some never saw King Street again. Others returned broken and languished without glory, to remain in veterans' hospitals for fifty years or more.

Oswald would have joined up as a chaplain, but he was unable to pass the army medical examination. Frailty and ill health had characterized his youth and Daisy later remembered the embarrassment, secret joy and relief she felt when she learned Oswald would remain in Toronto. This European war would not affect her, she had concluded shortly after her marriage.

By late 1916, life was beginning to settle for Daisy and Oswald. The initial adjustment to married life had been made, with reasonable success. Daisy was expecting her first child and Oswald was doing well at Dale. Notwithstanding Daisy's initial misgivings about his ability, which she had taken upon herself to reveal to Mr. Morrow, her husband seemed to have gained acceptance and was well established in the looming shadow of Toronto's most energetic pastor.

It was during dinner at the Morrow home, reminiscent of another fateful evening there, that the neatly ordered family life which Oswald and Daisy had established collapsed. Mr. Morrow was chatting amiably about his cottage and how he scarcely found time to go there any more. Without pausing he continued, "You'll soon know what I mean, Mr. Smith, for I've signed up as an army chaplain and I sail in two weeks' time. You've been appointed pastor at Dale, that is, if you'll accept."

It was so matter-of-fact. He might have been going around the corner for lunch and leaving Oswald to mind the store, rather than around the world to war.

Oswald was twenty-eight. His first full pastorate was not to be a small, sleepy congregation, but Dale Presbyterian Church! The awesome responsibility descended on him like a leaden mantle. Mr. Morrow continued to chatter away about his garden, the oil leak of his motorcycle and other even less significant things. Oswald sat stunned. Daisy had to deliver a firm elbow to his ribs to restore his attention. She knew that Morrow's decision would radically alter their life, that it was the most significant event in Oswald's ministry to date and that he would need her encouragement and support.

As they turned the corner of Garden Avenue later that evening, Oswald shook his head. "No, Daisy," he said. "How can I accept a full pastorate at Dale? I may have the training but I lack the spiritual depth that I feel I need to lead the people."

"Oswald, I feel God has opened this door and you must enter," Daisy advised. "You lack nothing which the indwelling Holy Spirit cannot supply if you yield your will to Him."

Daisy had spoken of the fullness of the Holy Spirit and the victorious life to be found in Him before. These were strange terms that Oswald had not been taught in the Presbyterian seminary as thoroughly as Daisy had at her Alliance Church and all during her Bible school days. If there was an experience of power which he had missed, he knew that he would need it now as never before to meet the challenge of Dale.

"I know you are a child of God," said Daisy, "but you are going to need the power of the Holy Spirit to gain victory over temptation. The Holy Spirit comes to dwell within us when we accept Christ, but, Oswald, we cannot keep one room of our hearts closed to Him. We must not reserve as much as a cupboard or closet for ourselves. We must yield every area of our lives to Him and His power will be translated into a more effective ministry."

Oswald listened attentively to all that Daisy had to say, and as they reached the house and entered he pressed her for more information on what she knew concerning the indwelling of the Holy Spirit. They continued to talk late into the night.

This began an important period of intense spiritual growth for Daisy and her husband. They discussed the indwelling of the Spirit at great length and prayed together continually. Oswald's thirst for spiritual growth was insatiable. He began long sessions of solitary prayer in the mornings, pacing to and fro in his study at home. His "morning watch" soon became an inflexible practice, one he was to keep ever after, and the Keswick message of the victorious life was included in his preaching and writing ministry during all the years that lay ahead. He made it one of the four main emphases of the world-famous church that he and Daisy were eventually to found.

Daisy brought her own childhood background and perspective on foreign missions to bear on these discussions. This too was of great interest to Oswald. As his spiritual experience deepened, his passion for foreign missions soared. Thus Daisy's two greatest contributions to his ministry came within the first year of their marriage. She introduced him to the teaching she had received concerning the Spirit-filled life, in the Alliance Church as a child, and later in Bible school. The Alliance Church had always emphasized foreign missions and with this background she strengthened the passion he had always had for foreign missionary work. These two aspects of Christian experience became inextricably entwined in Oswald's heart and upon these cornerstones his ministry was built.

The birth of their first child, a son whom they named Glen Gilmour, in June 1917, symbolically coincided with this great awakening in Oswald. Of course, he accepted the challenge at Dale. Before long his own deepening experience and keen interest in missions found expression in his ministry. His great zeal kept pressing in upon him; he became restless and felt inhibited at Dale Church to carry out what he thought was God's plan for his ministry. Some of the officials had gained their positions in the church because of lodge affiliations instead of spiritual qualifications. Oswald seemed to be having times of alternate victories and bitter defeat. Many were won to a knowledge of Christ, but at the same time he encountered much opposition. Though many supported him, he caused great offense to others by raising six hundred dollars for missions. He used gospel hymns instead of the old hymns of the Presbyterian Church and many objected. He and Daisy became discouraged, but, realizing that discouragement has its source in Satan, they carried on as they were forced more and more to lean on the Holy Spirit. Depressed and perplexed on returning home from a service, Oswald wrote in his diary: "September 2nd. Preached tonight. Had liberty and a little power. People at great tension. Searched their faces in vain for signs of soul anguish and distress. Eyes dry. No outward token of conviction. Surely, I am not yet endued with power from on high!" Being young and inexperienced, he decided to resign rather than fight on under such conditions.

Daisy and Oswald felt disappointed and sorry to have to give up their ministry at Dale where they had met each other and had had such a fruitful ministry, but where for a long time they had experienced a time of breaking of spirit and soul. It was extremely hard on Daisy to watch her gifted husband reduced to being an usher, trying to help in the Paul Rader campaign, then attempting to do personal work and being ignored. Finally he sold hymn books in the aisles while others sat on the platform. At times Daisy wondered if the calling of God to conduct a world-wide ministry from Toronto was all a dream.

She felt even more puzzled when he decided to sell their first little home to accept work among the lumber-jacks and Indians of British Columbia, planning to leave her and little Glen in Vancouver while he traveled by steamer to minister up the coast with his friend Dr. Hooper. He had left home when a boy of eighteen and taken the train to British Columbia to do missionary work. "How strange and how mysteriously our footsteps are ordered," Daisy thought, "to think that Oswald is returning to his first mission field all these years later." What would Vancouver be like? What would life be for Glen and her while he journeyed up the coast, traveling by steamer, logging train and, eventually, by canoe to get to his destination?

Daisy soon discovered that Vancouver, in 1917, was nothing more than a logging town by the sea surrounded by majestic mountains and dense forests. Their first task was to secure a place to live and with little money at their disposal, they decided on a basement apartment at a very low rent. Later, a small furnished house was available for fifty dollars a month and here Glen and Daisy stayed while Oswald took his trips up the coast. This was the first time they had parted since their marriage and Daisy found it another hard adjustment, though she did not realize it was the beginning of many more partings to follow. When a life is given over to God and His will, no one can say where He may lead; the important thing is to be willing to follow at any cost. Glen cried uncontrollably when his father left, and it took all the courage Oswald could muster to release the chubby little hands clasped tightly around his neck. Leaving home as a boy of eighteen seemed easier somehow than now having to leave his faithful wife and son whom he adored. As he stepped onto the steamer he knew this was God's will and He had brought them out to the forests of British Columbia for a purpose.

After many trips, the purpose for coming began to unfold in a most unexpected way. Oswald enjoyed his times of communion and waiting on God as he went deep into the dense forest with his friend Dr. Hooper to pray. The gigantic pine trees towered high into the blue of the sky above him, making him feel infinitely small and insignificant amidst such grandeur. Moss and ferns filled the forest floor. After praying with Dr. Hooper he wandered off alone deeper into the shelter of massive trees and knelt by a huge fallen log. It seemed as though he was kneeling at an altar, with shafts of light pouring down from heaven, piercing the long brilliant rays through the pillars, as it were, of this outdoor cathedral.

Suddenly, as he was in fervent prayer, he saw a vision of hundreds and hundreds of people in a huge building in Toronto—people for whom Jesus died, people who needed a Savior, people who needed a Shepherd. Instantly he envisioned himself as the shepherd that was to lead this great flock. Looking up into the heavens he thanked God for illuminating the way before him and calling him back to Toronto to obey His will. As the apostle Paul of old he prayed, "What wilt Thou have me to do?"

The same answer came back, "Arise and go into the city, and it shall be told thee what thou must do." God knew his heart and his willingness to serve Him, and though Oswald could not see ahead, he knew God was ordering his steps to the work He alone could see for him.

Traveling back down the coast he was wondering what Daisy would think when he related his experience. Would she ever understand why God had uprooted her and Glen and brought them away out here to Vancouver where they did not know anyone and where they had been so lonely for weeks at a time? He could hardly wait to catch sight of her standing on the dock with their tiny son to meet him. Yes, scanning the shoreline, in the distance he could see Glen, jumping up and down with excitement, waiting for him to step off the ship.

All the way to their modest rented home Oswald was telling Daisy of his rewarding work with the lumberjacks during the past month. From the time these trips began, he was always full of enthusiasm over what God had done through him, but this time he had more zeal and excitement about his work than ever before. Daisy did not fully know why until Glen had been tucked into bed that night and Oswald began to relate to her the vision God had given him in that unforgettable spot as he knelt in humility on the floor of fern by a fallen tree, which had represented to him an altar in the presence of the great Creator Himself.

Listening with deep interest she realized how real this vision was to Oswald. She had never thought of him as a visionary but she agreed that God Himself had spoken in this manner to him. Though she knew of no specific work to which they could return, she also knew to ignore

God's voice was impossible; therefore, they must in obedience leave for Toronto.

A typical drizzle soaked a fog-shrouded Vancouver as the young couple and their little son boarded the train for Toronto. The dreary morning magnified the gloom that uncontrollably gripped Daisy's heart. Taking Glen on her knee she looked at the high, snow-capped mountain peaks rising one after another before her. The sun shone on their summits making the snow glisten like myriads of diamonds. "How majestically the snowy crests resemble the joys and successes of our life," she mused. Then the train wandered down into shadowed valleys. Without the valleys the train could never have crossed to those rugged heights. In the valleys Daisy noticed scattered dwellings. Here the people lived and worked. "Indeed most of life is lived in the valley," she thought. Experiences and dreams glimpsed from the mountain peaks are worked out in the valleys. Slowly the train would struggle and strain to climb the steep slopes to the mountain top again. From this height could be seen a glorious panoramic view, unknown to those living in the lowlands.

As they left the mountains and valleys, the scene changed. They were crossing the prairie, uninteresting, flat and monotonous with no end in sight. Daisy thought as she looked into the distance how similar it was to her life at that moment. She was not at the mountain peak of life, enjoying success and the splendor she had once known. She was not even in the fertile valley occupied with a fruitful ministry. She had reached a wilderness with no apparent end. Life was uneventful, unvaried, with little meaning left. Would she ever emerge from this desert period? What was ahead for her? Should she have remained a deaconess, going about her tasks with enthusiasm, a zest for living, and a feeling of accomplishment in her ministry? She recalled how happy she was in those days with the work she loved and the freedom she had to make her own decisions. Would she ever feel that way again? Just then a tiny hand caught hold of her chin, interrupting her thoughts. The hand pulled her head around so that a precious little boy could kiss his mother.

"Oh, Glen," she thought, holding him closer, "I would never want to go back! With you and your father and our heavenly Father, we will see the end of this wilderness."

Not only did Daisy find herself in a personal wilderness upon returning to Toronto with no work for her husband in sight, a young son and another baby on the way, but when she picked up the newspaper shortly after their arrival, to her horror she read of the epidemic of influenza that was sweeping the whole world. Very few expectant mothers were spared if they contracted the disease. Her thoughts went to her sister Hazel who lived in the United States and was due to give birth to her third child momentarily.

Wondering how Hazel was, she was startled by a sharp knock at the door. "Telegram for Daisy Smith," announced the messenger boy as he placed it in her hands. Trembling, Daisy reached for it and hastened to open it. As she read her face grew pale with shock.

Hazel passed away this morning after giving birth to a son.
Signed
Godfrey.

"Hazel!" cried Daisy. "But she is only twenty-seven!

What will her children do without their beautiful, happy mother? Poor Godfrey. How can he manage all alone? Oh, God, and I thought I was in a wilderness!"

Oswald arrived home from conducting a funeral. Before Daisy had time to tell him about Hazel, he exclaimed, I have never seen anything like it! Graves cannot be dug quickly enough to bury the dead! Coffins are piled high everywhere! They say nearly twenty million people have died throughout the world already as a result of this influenza! We'll have to pray earnestly that God will spare you while you are carrying our second child." He was obviously very concerned about her, and she felt this was not the time to tell him about her beloved sister. Bravely, she assured him that her life was in God's hands and He would take care of her.

Two days later Daisy accompanied her mother to the train to meet Godfrey and his three motherless children. He had brought Hazel's body home to Toronto for burial. Mrs. Billings' heart was broken, but she took Godfrey and the children home with her where she continued to care for them.

When Daisy returned grief-stricken from Hazel's funeral the following day, she noticed Oswald's car in the driveway. "What is he doing home so early?" she wondered. He had several funerals to conduct and she did not expect to see him until much later.

"Oswald," she called, as she entered the house.

"I am lying down, Daisy. I felt so weak at the funeral I had to come home."

Daisy took one look at his flushed face as she entered the room, and decided to call his friend, Dr. Hooper, who had also returned from British Columbia to live in Toronto. When the doctor confirmed what she feared (that Oswald had contracted the dread disease), a feeling of utter despair overwhelmed her.

"His condition is serious, Mrs. Smith," he said, "and you cannot possibly nurse him. Although nurses are extremely scarce, I will do all that is in my power to secure one for you."

It was a miracle that Dr. Hooper was able to find Miss Millan, a capable nurse. Not only did she spend hours nursing Oswald, but she prepared meals, looked after the coal furnace and worked unceasingly around the clock with minimum rest.

A couple of days after she arrived, noticing that Glen was not his usual happy self, she took his temperature. Finding that it was soaring rapidly, she put him in the bed next to his father's and then went to break the news to Daisy. This was almost more than Daisy could bear. Nevertheless, despite her weakness, she helped Miss Millan prepare the mustard plasters for Glen's chest and kept them on him constantly in an attempt to relieve the congestion.

Miss Millan, exhausted with her duties, lay down on her bed to catch some much needed sleep. She was awakened by a loud moaning from Daisy's room. Jumping up and rushing to her side, she quickly realized that Daisy was in labor. She ran to the phone to call Dr. Hooper, only to find he was out on another case. Wearied in body herself, she stayed close by Daisy, encouraging her and helping all she could until the doctor finally arrived just as she was about to deliver the baby herself.

Hope Evangeline was born February 4, 1920, in the midst of a troubled, sick world. Daisy was so weak and anxious about her husband, who was not expected to live, and her son Glen, that she was disinterested in even looking at her baby girl for several days. One day when she was feeling a little stronger she told Miss Millan why they had decided to call the baby Hope Evangeline. She explained that she and Oswald were reading Longfellow's "Evangeline" together for weeks before her birth and thought it would make a beautiful name for the child if it should be a girl. "She is one ray of hope in this darkness," she said, "and that is why I want her first name to be Hope."

"If she turns out to be a writer like her father," replied Miss Millan, "Hope Evangeline would make a good pen name. Let us pray that God will spare her through this dreadful time and do just that," she continued as she bowed in prayer. Daisy never ceased to thank God for this devoted, spiritual nurse—a miraculous answer to a desperate situation.

After Miss Millan left the room to prepare the evening nourishment for her patients, Daisy, in all her weakness, decided to get out of bed and, holding on to the stair banister, made her way toward her husband's room. She was positive the doctor was keeping the truth from her and determined to see for herself. She had overheard Dr. Hooper talking to Miss Millan earlier. "There is very little hope for Glen," he had said in somber tones. Her heart filled with despair and utter hopelessness as she looked at them both struggling to breathe, their faces flushed with very high fevers. Slowly losing her grip on the stair banister, she fell to the floor in a dead faint. Miss Millan heard the thud, and flying up the stairs she hurried to Daisy and managed to lift her back to her bed. When Daisy returned to consciousness a little later, she looked up at faithful Miss Millan watching over her and asked, "Do you think we will ever see the end of this darkness, nurse?" Miss Millan assured her that God was faithful and would answer their fervent prayers for recovery.

Prayers were answered in a miraculous way; Glen and Oswald were finally pronounced out of danger. Glen was the first to recover. His Grandmother Smith came to take him to her house to lessen the burden of the family. He came into his mother's room to see his baby sister and to say good-bye to her. As he left, he kissed Daisy and looking up into her face, said pleadingly, "Don't die if you can help it, will you, Mother?"

With twenty million people losing their lives during the epidemic, Daisy realized their recovery was a miracle and felt more than ever God had spared their family for a definite purpose. They determined to find that purpose.

Oswald had not lost his vision of starting a great work in Toronto, but for several years it was very hard going, as they hit many rocks and reefs in the stormy seas of life. With nothing to start a work, their faith was sorely tried. Gradually God began to move in the hearts of various people to send gifts of money for the Lord's work and before long meetings were held in an auditorium in the Y.M.C.A. with a seating capacity of seven hundred and fifty.

From this building they moved on, renting larger and larger buildings as they tried to get a church established. Oswald never demanded any fixed amount as a salary and as a result they were forced to manage on a meager allowance, living completely by faith; but in a miraculous way every need was met.

During this time they were led to erect a large tent (90 feet square) on a corner in downtown Toronto. Oswald asked the people to bring their own chairs because he could not find two thousand chairs to fill the tent. Daisy marveled at the faith of her husband that people would bring their own chairs. Courageously, she got the children ready to leave for the first tent meeting. As they drew near the corner where the tent stood, her excitement mounted; she felt a sense of relief as she watched literally hundreds of people dismounting from one street car after another and carrying chairs of every description.

When the service began, the tent was filled and everyone was seated. The crowds continued to come every night of the campaign and many walked the saw-dust trail to accept Christ at the altar when the invitation was given at the conclusion of each service.

Daisy found it hard to get to the services every night as she was expecting her third child and Hope was just sixteen months old. On the first day of June 1921, her second son was born. They called him Paul Brainerd; after David Brainerd the missionary they both admired greatly; David Brainerd was known as the "Man of Prayer," and this name represented their aspirations for Paul.

Paul was a delicate child and suffered from severe convulsions when he was young. One day he looked up into his mother's anxious face during one of these convulsions, and heard her say to a friend standing by, "I have tried everything; I don't know of another thing I can do!"

A long silence followed and then the little fellow spoke up in his distress, "But you haven't prayed."

Daisy, feeling rebuked, confessed silently to God that she had lacked faith to pray for his recovery. He had suffered so many attacks. Now bowing her head she said,

"You pray for yourself, darling." In his simple, childlike way he asked Jesus to please stop his convulsions. From that day on, he never experienced another attack. God in His mercy answered the earnest prayer of a tiny, afflicted boy, and miraculously healed him. Daisy feared from the time he was born that God was going to take him to Himself, but from that day she never looked back and was convinced God was sparing him for a special purpose.

The time came at last when it was necessary to rent buildings for the services. Realizing the need for a permanent building, the Alliance Church made it possible to build a tabernacle seating two thousand, and Oswald became the pastor. They also provided five thousand dollars with which to purchase a small house for the young minister and his family.

Daisy, happy and thankful at last to be settled in a church home appreciated the Alliance people who believed strongly in missions. The work prospered continually until the building had to be enlarged.

After some time in the new church, Oswald returned home from a missionary meeting at which his friend Pastor William Fetler from Russia had challenged the congregation to commence missions in Russia. Daisy was getting the children ready for bed, singing happily and thanking God in her heart for straightening the crooked roads before them and blessing their days with smooth sailing in the ministry. Oswald entered the room with a lively step, eyes sparkling with enthusiasm, and in an excited voice told his contented wife that Pastor Fetler had invited him to visit the mission fields of Russia.

"Russia! Oh!" she exclaimed, trying to conceal the

shock. "That is wonderful! This will be the first time you have seen a foreign mission field! How long will you be away?"

"I sail from Quebec City where we had our honeymoon, and Pastor Fetler says it will take all of six months to complete the trip."

"Six months!" Daisy already felt waves of loneliness sweeping over her at the thought of spending months without Oswald to share the burdens and responsibilities of home and church.

Then looking away from her husband she turned to the children. "Time to say our prayers, children," she said as she tried to regain her composure.

After the children were safely tucked into bed she sat down in the living room in the big chair opposite Oswald. "Oswald," she began, "I am happy for you. I will pray every day that God will give you a new vision of missions that will inspire our people. I just have one prayer request."

"Tell me, that I might join you in prayer, Daisy."

"I wish you would pray that God would send me a young girl to help with the children while you are away so that I can do my share at the church. You know I always have the speakers for dinner on Sunday. I like them to feel at home but with the children it is becoming hard to meet the demands of the church and be sure their needs are met as well."

"Let us pray about that right now. I would feel happier if I knew you were not entirely alone." Together they knelt in prayer and made her request known to their heavenly Father.

A few weeks later Oswald announced to the congregation that he would be away for six months on a missionary trip to Russia. He preached a powerful sermon and many young people accepted Christ as Savior. At the close of the service Chrissie French, a young Irish girl, shook hands with Daisy. With tears of joy filling her blue eyes, she told Daisy that she had just become a Christian. She said she had a great desire to be of help to Daisy as she loved children and would like nothing better than to look after them and assist with the housework. She would look upon this as her ministry—something she could do for God.

Daisy did not have to stop to consider Chrissie's proposal. She knew this was an answer to prayer. She was overjoyed while driving home in the car that night to be able to tell Oswald that God had sent them a helper. Chrissie was going to move in and assist her. Little did Daisy know then that Chrissie would still be with her forty-three years later, serving faithfully. What an answer to prayer!

The day came for Oswald to leave and Daisy bravely, along with the children, waved good-bye until the train carrying him to Quebec to board the ship was out of sight. The Lord gave her a beautiful verse from His Word as she started for home— I Samuel 30:24 (" . . . so shall his part be that tarrieth by the stuff: they shall part alike"). She was convinced her role in fulfilling the Great Commission was to stay with her children and pray for her husband, supporting the work in his absence. Without the love, security and backing of a Christian wife like Daisy, Oswald could never have accomplished such exploits for God.

On the very day he had left Daisy was awakened at midnight by a distressing phone call from one of the church members.

"Is Dr. Smith there, please?" sobbed the lady on the other end. "I am in terrible trouble and I want to speak to him."

"I am sorry, Dr. Smith just left for Russia a few hours ago. Is there anything I can do?" asked Daisy. It was Mrs. Baker, a Christian woman that had been stricken with polio after her children were born. She was in a wheelchair continually, unable to keep house. Her husband was not a Christian. She seemed to be in agony, and Daisy was besieged with questions that gushed forth from a heart overwrought with what appeared to be insurmountable problems.

"But, Mrs. Smith," she said in a trembling voice, "you do not seem to understand! Why is God allowing me to suffer so much when I am His child? I have been a Christian so long!"

"Suffering comes in various forms. This is the way it has come to you, Mrs. Baker, but others suffer in different ways which you perhaps do not see. The Bible is filled with stories of Christians tested in one way or another. We enter the kingdom through much tribulation; we must trust His Word as to the reason. We are not here to drift and dream. We have to believe that God has promised to complete the pattern of our lives, sometimes through suffering, to bring us closer to Him."

Mrs. Baker then told Daisy that her drunken husband had left her locked in her room. She had managed to maneuver her wheelchair to the phone to call Dr. Smith.

"Oh, dear, I had better call the police," exclaimed Daisy. "They will be able to break the lock and help you. I will come also and pray with you."

When Daisy called the police, she asked them to pick her up on the way. While dressing and waiting for them to arrive, she began praying for Mrs. Baker, turning back and forth in her mind the age-old question of why Christians suffer. As she knelt down by her bed, her anxious heart grew still before God in prayer. She asked Him, "But why do some people have to suffer so much more than others?" She had never endured hardship like Mrs. Baker's. Then it seemed she heard God's voice saying in His gentle, comforting tones, "I fit the back for the burden. The surgeon has to hurt and dig deep sometimes to restore a perfect body. Nevertheless, it is all worthwhile, and the reason some have more pruning and testing than others is that I alone know those particular individuals who can bear it. In the end they will come out as pure gold, fit for the kingdom. They will stand perfect before me. I cannot put some through such fervent heat," He seemed to say, "because they would melt away under it, but to those who endure to the end is promised a great reward."

The doorbell rang as Daisy rose from her knees. She joined the police who were on their way to Mrs. Baker.

Reaching the bedroom door, they could hear her sobbing. The police broke the lock and opened the door. Daisy walked toward the distraught woman and, placing her arm lovingly around her in an attempt to comfort her, noticed she was becoming much quieter. While she had been waiting for Daisy to arrive, God had revealed to this anguished soul why she, as a Christian, had to endure such bitter pain. He had answered her questions just as He had answered similar ones for Daisy while she was in prayer.

Just then, Mr. Baker returned. Glancing wildly in Daisy's direction, he screamed, "What are you doing

A Selection
from
DAISY'S
PHOTO ALBUM

*Elizabeth McIntyre,
Daisy's Grandmother*

*Minnie Billings,
Daisy's Mother*

Daisy at Age Nine

Daisy and Ada at Nyack

Leaving for West Virginia

Daisy, the Deaconess

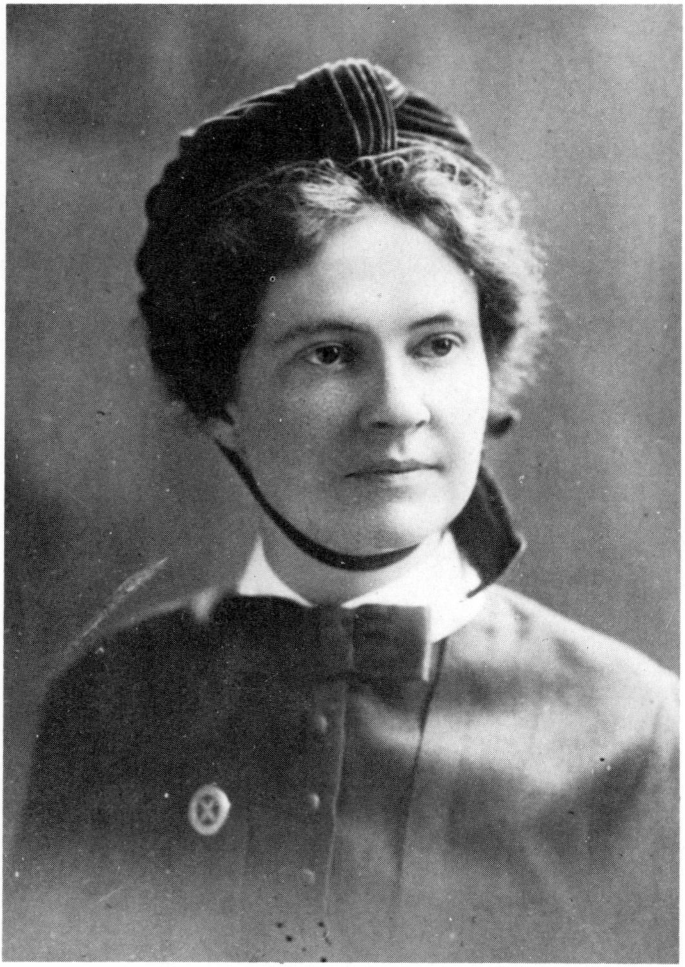

Deaconess Training Home (Daisy is second from right, second row from back)

Daisy at Dale

The Honeymoon

Only A Ring.
Dedicated to Daisy

'Twas only a ring that I gave you, dear,
'Neath the light of the stars so true,
And oh, it seemed such a little thing —
But it sealed, it sealed our love!
Then wear it, dear, while the years go by —
My own true love forever;
And from that hour that made us one
May naught arise to sever!

'Twas only a ring, yes, only a ring
That I placed upon your hand
But you must not think of the value, dear,
Or your heart would understand.
For it takes us back to the hallowed spot
Where first we told the story,
And it bears us on to the coming years —
The promise of love's glory!

'Twas only a ring, but it told you, dear,
Of a love that would not die,
Away in the woods by the river side,
And under the star-lit sky.
With never a sound but the paddle drips,
And the murmur of voices low —
Or the tender strains of a plaintive song
As the boats passed to & fro.

'Twas only a ring, but the night throbbed on,
And it seemed so hard to part;
For the mystic spell of a joy unknown
Had stolen upon your heart.
Then wear it, dear, while the years go by —
My own true love forever;
And from that hour that made us one
May naught arise to sever!

Oswald C. J

June 1 & 2/16.

Original Copy of "Only A Ring" in Oswald's Handwriting

Daisy, Young Mother

Garden Rest

Glen, Daisy's First Child

Chrissie and Paul

Glen and Oswald in Vancouver

Glen, Hope, and Paul

With Kaola Bears in Australia

Enjoying a Swiss Villa in Chile

*Daisy and Oswald on TV for
World Literature Crusade*

Daisy Turning the Sod

Laying of the Cornerstone

Final Day on Bloor Street

Peoples Church on Sheppard Avenue

1969 World Missions Conference at Peoples Church

Daisy and Family on Golden Wedding Anniversary

Front row (l. to r.): Ruth, Don, Violet, Cress. Back Row: Daisy and Mother

Golden Wedding Anniversary

here?" Then pointing to his wife he added, "There she is, an invalid, paralyzed, no use to me or anyone else, and she is supposed to be a Christian! I married a beautiful young bride whom I thought would make me happy and be able to look after my home and family, but what did I get? If that is how God treats His so-called children who believe in Him," he roared, glaring at his wife, "I want nothing to do with Him. It's a farce! She reads her Bible every day, prays, goes to your church, and look at her! What good is it all? I'm fed up with this Christianity! Christians have to suffer more than other people it seems to me." When he had concluded his raging outburst before Daisy and his tortured wife, Daisy tried to explain to him why Christians often suffer, as God had revealed the answer to her.

"All right, but why do I have to suffer then? I am not a Christian, and I sure did not ask for all this trouble. I provide for my family and I would have been a good husband and father if it had not been for all this. He doesn't have to perfect me for heaven. I'm not even counting on going," he roared with a voice consumed with terrible bitterness.

"Mr. Baker," said Daisy in her calm, loving and gracious manner, "I believe your suffering has been earned by your own willfulness to live apart from God. It is your fault and no one else is to blame. God has nothing to do with it since you have never gone to Him for help. Yet you reprove Him for it. You must bear the suffering your sins have caused."

Though Daisy believed what she had said to him, she feared he would be furious. Instead he absorbed her words and thought about them. Feeling the sting of the reproach she had given him, he bowed his head. Daisy's words had been powerful and spoken with strong conviction, but Mr. Baker also felt the love and compassion in her voice. His wife grasped the arms of her wheelchair with her bruised hands. She had a deep, ugly gash across the forehead where he in his drunken rage had struck her before he locked her in the room and left. This was all forgotten as she observed a gradual change in her husband's countenance.

He raised his head and, looking Daisy straight in the eye, said, "Tell me something! When you have suffered in one way or another, how do you feel about God?"

"I never think of blaming God," replied Daisy. "I know I have failed somewhere and my only desire is to get closer to Him and see where I went wrong. Occasionally, if I wait long enough, I see the reason for my suffering, although sometimes I never see the reason. I know nothing happens to us without a purpose, because God's Word says in Romans 8:28 that 'all things work together for good.' I am satisfied to believe His Word and leave the reason for suffering to Him."

Mr. Baker's enraged expression became submissive and peaceful. "I want to believe in Him too," he admitted in subdued tones. "You are right; I have never thought of asking Him to help me, and I have insisted on living apart from Him." His voice almost broke with emotion, "I want to trust Him tonight, Mrs. Smith. I see I have been wrong."

After she had led him to the Lord, Mr. Baker graciously called a taxi to take Daisy home. Her heart was filled to overflowing to think that he had found Christ as His Savior. God used his wife's call for help to accomplish his salvation. "All things do work together for good," repeated Daisy as she settled down to sleep in the early hours of the morning.

Daisy looked forward to letters from Russia, although most of her husband's letters were like telegrams mentioning only the highlights in brief. One letter, however, written shortly after he arrived, impressed her deeply as he had enclosed a verse of a poem he had written—later set to music:

> Russia, dark Russia,
>   Land of sorrow, sin and night;
> No Christ, no Savior
>   And no gospel light;
> I have seen the vision,
>   And for self I cannot live;
> Life is less than worthless
>   Till my all I give.
>   (1924)

Every night after supper, the children took turns at family worship praying for their father. They attended church regularly and Daisy had to learn how to manage everything concerned with the house as if she were a widow. She continued with these responsibilities even when her husband was home, keeping the children from his study door when he was praying, preparing sermons, writing hymns or books, so that they would not disturb him. Daisy did everything in her power to reserve his energies and time for God's work. As a result, replacing a blown fuse or repairing any household item was foreign to him. His work for God came first in Daisy's mind as well as in his.

At last the day came when he arrived home from Russia, his first real missionary trip! Daisy took the three children to meet him at the old Union station and, filled with enthusiasm concerning all he had witnessed, he related his experiences. Chrissie had placed "Welcome Home" signs all over the house and though he had enjoyed a thrilling trip, he was glad to be back eating Canadian food again, and sleeping in his own bed.

Oswald settled down in the Alliance Church work again for some time, until the day came when he felt, for various reasons, he should resign as pastor and branch out into evangelistic campaigns throughout the United States, presenting to churches everywhere a new method of missionary giving. He had seen the vision and the mission fields constantly drew him as a magnet. Daisy was puzzled at the way God was leading him and she was even more bewildered when he accepted another pastorate in Los Angeles, California. She recalled the graphic vision God had given him of a great work in Toronto. And now, just when the vision was realized, all became a dream again. To her at the time it seemed calamitous and unreasonable but, realizing God's ways are higher than our ways and past finding out with our finite minds, she clung to Psalm 138:8—"The Lord will perfect that which concerneth me. . . ." It was not His time. As she had been taught, she had to "wait patiently for Him."

The Smith family was not in Los Angeles more than a week when Oswald became restless and realized Toronto was where he belonged after all. God enabled him to raise ten thousand dollars for the work in Russia during the year and his ministry was greatly appreciated, so Daisy felt they had not strayed from the will of God by accepting that pastorate.

A Russian prima donna sang whenever Oswald brought Pastor Fetler and others to challenge the people of Los Angeles concerning missionary work. One night the soloist had a bad cold and was unable to sing.

"In the prima donna's place tonight I am going to have my younger son, Paul, sing for you," announced Oswald. Paul was now five years old and had an unusual voice for a small boy. Daisy had made him a black satin suit trimmed with a white collar and cuffs, a white satin vest, and short black pants. A mop of long golden curls that Daisy refused to cut, his deep dimples and fine features, made him look more like a girl than a boy. His actions, however, were every bit those of a boy.

When he was dressed, ready to go to the church to sing to about two thousand people, he disappeared. Suddenly, Daisy heard him calling, "Help me, I'm stuck, I can't get down!" Looking out the window, she saw him hanging by his black satin pants from the top of a high barbed wire fence that surrounded the cemetery across from the house. Chrissie ran to rescue him and to her horror saw that he had ripped the seat of his pants from top to bottom. When Oswald saw them, all he could say was, "Don't take time to remove them. We are late. Put him over your knee and sew them up!" He then got into the car and waited impatiently, honking the horn at intervals in hopes it would hurry them out. Rushing to the car they managed to get Paul to the platform just in time for his first number.

As this tiny boy, looking like Little Lord Fauntleroy, rose to sing, an artist sitting in the congregation turned to his wife and whispered, "I have seen the model I want to paint. I wonder if they would give me permission to do his portrait?" Austin Shaw, a well-known California artist, had painted many famous people, charging no less than about three thousand dollars.

Paul sang, as he stood on a stool so that he could be seen, "I'm Going Higher Some Day." He had a big voice for his small body and was called "The Golden Voice Soloist" by the newspapers. Much to Mr. Shaw's delight, after the service he obtained permission to paint Paul's portrait. This portrait served as the cover page on the *Fine Arts Magazine* for the following year. It hung in many art galleries and later he presented it to the family. This portrait was one of Daisy's prized possessions as long as she lived. To her it was a picture of a miracle because it portrayed God's purpose for a life she feared at one time would be snuffed out. Whenever she looked at the picture she thought of the early age at which Paul ministered in song on the platform, destined to be used of God for the rest of his life.

Though the church board pleaded with Oswald to stay in California, offering to build a church seating three thousand people, he could not erase his vision of a work in Toronto from his mind, and in the month of May the whole family and Chrissie left by car for home. The highways were not finished in many places and the car gave endless trouble as they crossed the stifling hot Arizona desert, taking twelve days to drive three thousand miles. To add to the harassing trip, Hope developed the mumps, and became very sick. Finally they reached Toronto, exhausted, but glad to be again in the city where they felt God had called them. They could have stayed in California with a comfortable pastorate, but returned to Toronto without a church in which to start a permanent ministry.

Many urged Oswald to build a church, but he did not believe in debt or large mortgages.

It was 1929 and the country was plunged into the midst of the Great Depression. The stock market had crashed and money was scarce. People could not afford entertainment in those days and so it was easy to get large crowds to attend church. Services with good preaching and bright singing uplifted spirits in such darkness and uncertainty, but to raise money to build was impossible.

To the surprise of everyone, one Sunday morning Oswald made a startling announcement in the church he was renting. He said that he had been walking the floor in prayer, asking God to fulfill his dream of a permanent work in Toronto. "If someone would give us a gift of $10,000 as a start," he declared, "I would consider buying a church." With the country going through such a financial setback, many felt this was an outrageous proposal. For the following six years it was necessary to go on renting.

To have to wait so long to get settled was a trial of Daisy's faith, but God taught her many lessons of patience. She learned that He never shows us the finished picture. Only He knows the end at the very beginning; as His children we must obediently walk in His way. During that waiting period she relied on Genesis 24:27—". . . being in the way, the Lord led me. . . ." She knew from past experience that God's will is not always our will. When she left Nyack she became a missionary in West Virginia, but when the Lord led her into the Presbyterian Church she followed in obedience. She never would have met her husband if she had not allowed herself to be in the way the Lord would lead her. God was the Creator of the picture of her life. Daisy was simply the frame around the picture He was creating.

Through the trial of patience and faith she also learned that *complete* abandonment to God is necessary. Our own will must not interfere. We must not try to assist God, but must allow Him to have full control regardless of the cost even if His will appears unreasonable. Eventually she found that if she was patient she would hear His voice saying, "This is the way, walk ye in it."

She had been thinking seriously about whether it had really been the will of God to leave California where they had a lovely home and church, to take the children out of school to start again in new schools, and to give up all the security they could have had. Oswald, unaware of her feelings and thoughts at the time, walked into the room where she was meditating and handed her a poem:

Thy Will

O Lord, fulfill Thy will,
   Be the days few or many, good or ill;
Prolong them, to suffice
   For offering up ourselves Thy sacrifice;
Shorten them if Thou wilt,
   To make in righteousness an end of guilt.
Yea, they will not be long
   To souls who learn to sing a patient song;
Yea, short they will not be,
   To souls on tiptoe to flee home to Thee.
O Lord, fulfill Thy will,
   Make Thy will ours, and keep us patient still,
Be the days few or many, good or ill.

Christina Rossetti

Daisy resolved in her heart to make God's will her will, to show forth in her life the patience so aptly described in that poem.

7

A Break in the Clouds

Special weekly prayer meetings were being held asking God for a permanent church home, when Oswald, driving along Bloor Street, one of the main streets running east and west in the city, noticed a large church for sale with a seating capacity of about eighteen hundred. Stopping his car he got out to have a look at the auditorium and inquire. Everything about it suited him except the selling price of seventy-five thousand dollars. However, he was able to make arrangements to rent it from the United Church of Canada and the congregation, which he had built up in the old church at 42 Gerrard Street, East, moved to the Bloor Street location. Without a substantial down payment, which he did not have, it was entirely out of his reach to buy the church, that is, apart from a miracle of God.

One day when he returned home from his day at the office, still wishing he could buy the Bloor Street church, Daisy met him at the door and told him that Mr. Jaffray, the publisher of the *Globe* newspaper in the city, had called to see if they could have dinner at his home that evening.

"You know I would rather eat at home always, Daisy, but it was kind of him to invite us. What time is dinner?"

"Six o'clock, and, Oswald, I don't know why I feel as I do, but I think you will be glad you went and talked to this man of God. We have been praying for a long time and I feel encouraged. I have no concrete reason for my conviction, but I think we are on the brink of something wonderful just about to happen."

"What makes Daisy so encouraged?" thought Oswald as he prepared to leave for the Jaffray home. "She seems so happy about this dinner engagement. That intuition of hers is worth heeding. I wonder what it means this time. I feel nothing, but she is usually right when she gets an impression like the one she has tonight. Oh, well, soon we shall see what it is all about," he thought, deciding to say nothing to her about the impossible dream he had just seen.

When they were seated around the dining room table which was laden with a sumptuous meal, Mr. Jaffray began speaking. "You know, Dr. Smith, with the work you have built, and the tremendous following you have in this city, you desperately need to purchase a large church adequate for your needs," he said as though he were the first to become aware of this fact.

"I agree," said Oswald emphatically. "I have been praying for a permanent church for a long time, but we could not possibly go ahead without a substantial gift as a down payment."

"What would you consider a substantial gift?"

"The church on Bloor Street is for sale for seventy-five thousand dollars but I could not think of buying it unless I had at least ten thousand dollars as a down payment."

Daisy, looking at her husband, could hardly believe her ears. She thought he might suggest five thousand, but ten! No wonder Mr. Jaffray let the matter drop and changed the subject. "If only Oswald had given him a more reasonable figure!" she thought.

On the way home Daisy told him that he expected far too much. "I had a strong feeling Mr. Jaffray was interested in helping us before we went to his home, but I am afraid you have discouraged him," she said, looking utterly disappointed.

"Daisy, as the old saying goes—'Why ask for a cupful when the ocean remains?' All things are possible with God," he said confidently.

The next day was Sunday. Daisy, sitting with Chrissie and the children, looked around the church that they had been renting, and thought, "Why does God not hear us, and give us a church of our own? Why do we have to keep going from church to church never getting settled? We have waited and prayed for so long. God has prospered and blessed our work, but still our dream is not realized," she thought with a sigh.

With all these questions spinning around in her mind the following day, suddenly the phone rang. It was Mr. Jaffray. "Is your husband there?" he asked.

"No, Mr. Jaffray, but he should be back shortly," she replied. Her curiosity was aroused.

"Well, I want you to give him a message. Would you tell him that I have been much in prayer since both of you were here for dinner the other night, and the Lord has laid it upon my heart to give you $20,000 toward the purchase of that church that is for sale."

"Twenty thousand dollars!" she exclaimed, making sure she had heard the amount correctly.

"Yes, that is right. I feel definitely that this is the amount I am to give him, and I hope he will go ahead."

When Oswald returned, Daisy could hardly wait to tell him the good news. He was thrilled beyond words. "You were right as usual, Daisy; we are at the beginning of great things. Think of it! A gift of $20,000 from one individual!" Sitting down in the big chair to recover from the exciting news, Oswald saw once more the vision he had had while kneeling by the fallen log in British Columbia—a crowded auditorium in Toronto and people turned away because the seats were all taken an hour before the service was to start. He heard once more the bright singing of that crowd and saw souls streaming to the altar to accept Christ as Savior under his ministry. What was then a dream was now reality at last!

The Peoples Church, as they called it, was situated at 100 Bloor Street East on a strategic corner in downtown Toronto. Street cars bringing people from east and west stopped in front of the church doors. It was quite common in those days for the conductor of the car to call out, "Peoples Church, everybody off," as the car almost completely emptied in front of the church.

The highlight of the church calendar was the annual missionary convention, for which in later years it became world-famous. The anticipation and suspense of that time were an unparalleled experience. Just as every range of mountains has its high peaks, so in the hills of spiritual experience and service, one high peak rises above all others, and that was in April of each year at the convention.

Oswald taught the people to give a faith promise offering for the missionaries. It was a promise between themselves and God as to what they could trust God to enable them to give month by month in the coming year. He had started the first convention in the church on Gerrard Street with apprehension and yet a joyous anticipation as faith in God gripped hearts to believe Him for that first goal of $28,000 in 1935. This increased to $36,000 the next year and $43,372 ten years later.

"It is an enormous amount to expect," thought Daisy. At first the people did not know what it meant to give by faith. Oswald had been to the mission fields and seen the need, but she wondered if the congregation could catch the vision, and understand the necessity to give. But Oswald's faith was strong. He purposed in his heart from the first that he should not ask the people to do something he was not prepared to do himself and always set the example in his own giving. Together they prayed about the amount they would trust God to enable them to give, and after agreeing on it, would sign a faith promise envelope.

Little did they realize then the goodness of God to those who obey Him. Just as one casts that little pebble into a pond, and watches the ripples widen out farther and farther, increasing more and more, until the boundaries become limitless, so they cast their first small gift into God's great harvest field of missions, not dreaming how widely the work would expand and how great the harvest become. Neither did they comprehend then that the first goal in The Peoples Church would be multiplied under God to the unthinkable amount of one million dollars annually!

Daisy's heart and soul were in the work from its inception, literally living missions along with her husband, carrying the burden of the work with him as if they were one person. She felt a great strain and responsibility each year through the convention until the total was finally announced at the end and the choir triumphantly sang the "Hallelujah Chorus" in praise to God for what had been accomplished. At this climax on the last Sunday, tears of joy and gratitude to God always coursed down her cheeks.

The children enjoyed the missionaries' slides and exhibits as well as the bright singing of the Claus Indian family that came year after year wearing their colorful Indian costumes. When Paul was still a young boy he tried to think of a way he could earn money to pay his faith promise to the missionaries. His cousin came to visit him and showed him how to make humbug candies. Paul tied up bags of these candies he had made, and had a little stand at the entrance to the exhibit room where the people gathered after the service for fellowship with the missionaries over a cup of tea and sandwiches. All who passed by him could hardly resist buying a bag, especially when they knew he had made the candy himself to help keep his promise to the missionaries. All three children were taught to give something to missions each month, although Hope and Glen were not as enterprising as Paul in making an income. He had an irresistible way of persuading people to patronize his humbug stand. Looking back Daisy realized God prepared Paul at an early age to raise money for missions.

No doubt because missions came first, God looked after all other needs. Daisy often quoted Matthew 6:33, one of her favorite promises—"Seek ye first the kingdom of God and His righteousness; and all these things shall be added unto you." This verse became a reality in her life, time after time. No luxurious carpets covered the floors of the church and the same old cushions remained in the pews. The church walls were left unpainted so that the missionaries would always receive their allowances. But God wonderfully undertook as the church was bought and paid for within five years, and continued to increase in value. Missionary giving increased in spite of having to meet the payments for the church, and many new missionaries went out in service each year.

The Smith children were in their early teens now, and Paul and Glen shared a bedroom. One night Daisy heard them talking. Glen said, "You know, Paul, Dad expects one of us to be a minister."

"Yes, I know," replied Paul.

After a long pause, Glen continued, "Well, I could never be one," and rolling over in his bed, pulled the covers up. With a definite finality in his voice he added, "So, I guess it's up to you." Paul referred to this brief conversation in later years as his first call to the ministry.

Glen finished high school and entered the university to become a medical doctor. Paul left for a Christian college in the southern states when he had completed high school, since at the time there was no fundamental liberal arts college in Canada where he could begin training for the ministry. He spent several years in this fine school until the Second World War broke out in 1939. He returned to Canada and in the following three years studied at three different liberal schools. During this time, Daisy discovered he was losing his faith. He no longer read the Bible or spent time in prayer and became doubtful about all that he had been taught about the Bible since childhood. He majored in philosophy, and because he could not prove everything in the Bible scientifically, he began to look upon the miracles and truths it contained as simply myths, and questioned the authenticity of the inspired Word.

Daisy's heart was broken to think this had happened to Paul, the one she had hoped would be able to take over The Peoples Church some day. She had always been convinced God had spared and trained him from childhood to do a work for Him, and now she was saddened and crushed.

Brokenhearted, disappointed and bewildered, Daisy unburdened her heart to Oswald, telling him of the great change she had observed in Paul of late.

"The only thing we can do about this is take it to the Lord in prayer constantly until we see the answer," said Oswald equally disturbed and grieved. For many months, they, along with Chrissie, their devoted prayer partner, joined two and three times a day in prayer for Paul that he might find his faith again, and fulfill God's plan for his life.

Daisy likened this agonizing prayer for victory in Paul's life to the Battle of Britain that was raging at the time. "You know," she said to Oswald one day just before they commenced to pray, "when one is fighting a battle, he does not go around trying to defeat all the countries; he concentrates on the enemy until his armies have fought through to victory." She knew that to obtain a victorious answer to their prayers would require constant emphasis and concentration on that specific need. She had learned through years of intercessory prayer that one has to be specific.

At that time it seemed as if the heavens were brass. Though they interceded for weeks in prayer, Paul was growing farther and farther away from God. Feeling discouraged and troubled because Paul had not been coming home from the school as many weekends as he used to, and wondering why her prayer had not been answered yet, Daisy decided to take a promise from the little promise box that she kept beside her bed. She opened it and read Habakkuk 2:3—"... through it tarry, wait for it; because it will surely come." Wanting additional assurance she picked a second promise, which read, "Rest in the Lord and wait patiently for him..." (Psalm 37:7). Just then she heard the front door open and Paul's voice calling, "Mother, are you home?"

Quickly Daisy ran to the door, and though he was a man, she called out in her customary way, "It's the baby!" Embracing him, she expressed her joy at seeing him again after so many weeks.

"How is school?" she asked.

"It's all right, I guess, Mother," he said. "But I have decided not to write my master's thesis.

A little taken aback, Daisy exclaimed, "O Paul, you have studied so hard; it would be a shame not to get it now!"

"If you insist that I write it, Mother, I am afraid that you do not know what you are asking."

Daisy thought of the promise the Lord had just given her and suddenly realized that He had answered her prayers. Paul had no desire to write things he no longer believed, things he had been taught at college, and were not in accordance with the teachings of the Bible. He had found his faith in God and believed in His inspired Word once more. Much thought and study had driven him to the Scriptures and he had learned that one is not expected to prove the truths of the Bible, but to accept by faith what God has done in sending His Son to die on Calvary for our sins. Daisy often wondered why Paul had to go through such a bitter experience but realized in later years how invaluable it had been to him so that in dealing with young people in the future he might advise them and save them from similar pitfalls in their Christian lives. She gradually saw that the devil knew the great work Paul was destined to accomplish and had tried for four years in every conceivable way to overthrow him.

Paul was ordained in a Baptist church and went into evangelistic work, traveling extensively throughout Canada, the United States, and many other places, looking after spiritual needs everywhere; on the other hand, Glen, a devoted Christian, had obtained his medical degree and had joined the armed forces, doing what he could to alleviate the physical needs of mankind.

It was a bitter cold winter's day. Snow covered every bare branch standing out against the dreary gray of the sky. Strong north winds whipped the snow in gusts, picking it up and depositing it down again in deep drifts. Reports were coming over the radio concerning the war that was still raging. The allies at that time were suffering many setbacks. It seemed the war would never end. Glen was away in military service. Paul was preaching in his evangelistic meetings; the war had even taken Daisy's only daughter off to Vancouver, far from home with her husband who was in the air force. Daisy was almost overcome with gloom as she reviewed in her mind the darkness and loneliness engulfing her on every side.

As if this were not enough, Oswald came bounding in, interrupting her dreary thoughts, absolutely filled with enthusiasm and joy. Typically oblivious to everything that was taking place around him, untouched by everyday circumstances, and with a great buoyancy in his voice, he announced he was going to visit the head-hunters of the Solomon Islands. If he had said he was going to Florida or some other sunny, cheerful spot, Daisy might have joined him, but to the cannibals! "How foolish!" she thought. Few white men ever dared to venture a trip to such a dangerous place.

News of that nature was a little more than Daisy could bear. "Oswald!" she exclaimed. "Are you sure you haven't lost your head? If you haven't, I'm certain you will." With a knowing smile, a twinkle in his dancing blue eyes, and the ever present wanderlust in his heart, he replied, as he kissed her affectionately, "Now, Daisy, you should know by now, I have to follow the dictates of my heart, even if I lose my head." Then becoming more serious he asked, "Why should anyone hear the gospel twice before everyone has heard it once?"

The day arrived when Oswald set sail once more, this time for a long and arduous missionary trip to the Solomon Islands, Australia, and New Zealand, leaving various evangelists and Bible teachers in his pulpit during his absence.

Things were going well at the church and time was slipping by much faster than Daisy had anticipated. She was beginning to see a bright opening in the ominous clouds of winter as she looked forward to Oswald's return in just a few more weeks. Suddenly the bright horizon was darkened by the most alarming news. A cable was delivered to her which contained the following message: "Dr. Smith dangerously ill with malaria fever. Please ask church to pray."

Her first thought was to share this news with the children, but then, she was not sure exactly how to get in touch with them. After having prayer with Chrissie, she decided to round up as many as she could to come to a special prayer meeting that night. Knowing how frail her husband was, she was afraid he would never survive in the Solomon Islands without proper care. He usually became sick when he was traveling in foreign lands but this time she realized the sickness was of a more serious nature, and he was so far away from medical help. Many prayer meetings were held and at last she received another cable which said that he had recovered sufficiently to sail for home. He was never content to remain at home for long because of his undying, burning desire to do missionary work. Daisy understood to some extent his passion for souls, because she had a missionary heart also.

All during his absence she often longed to see the countries for which she had prayed, but felt she had an important and necessary task at home in the church. She was almost jealous of the work and its welfare when her husband was away, watching over every aspect of it with loving interest and care. To her it was like her child whom she had nurtured from birth.

She possessed a God-given perception and insight into church problems and people. Her words of wisdom often saved Oswald from making serious mistakes and wrong decisions. He loved and respected this quality in her and readily accepted her advice. She did not believe that ministers' wives should try to run everything in the church. Many in the congregation wanted to teach, sing in the choir, play the organ or piano, or conduct the prayer meetings, and she strongly advocated pushing the church members forward into these positions that they might experience the joy found in serving Jesus.

She conducted a Bible class but when it became larger and larger, she handed it to another capable woman to teach. She anticipated the danger of its becoming a little church within the church. As the minister's wife she wanted to contribute toward the whole congregation, not just concentrate on one corner of the church. It was not that she felt ministers' wives should not use their talents, but she learned from her days as a deaconess the danger of depriving others of doing service for God also.

She graciously welcomed strangers with a warm handshake and made a habit of entertaining visiting evangelists and missionaries in her home, feeling it important to let them enjoy the warmth of Christian hospitality. Meeting these men of God enriched the lives of her children as well. If she was needed by visitors or strangers the ushers could locate her as she always sat in the same pew. Her steadfast, faithful attendance and concern for the church gave her husband a security when he was absent, especially since he knew that because of her intense interest she would contact him if anything was amiss or needed his attention.

He was away so much of the time that Daisy felt a great responsibility and pressure, but never stood in the way of his convictions to make more and more missionary journeys. One time she could count on his being at home was Christmas and this was always a happy time for her and the family. She and Chrissie prepared a beautiful buffet for the whole family each Christmas night and Oswald's part was to show his movies of recent trips. Family movies taken long ago always brought gales of laughter from the group as they looked at action-packed films of too many people, doing too many things, too fast—Oswald's idea of making the most of expensive film left over from world tours.

He enjoyed having his family and friends come, but he, anything but a party man, also enjoyed bidding them farewell. When he had had enough of the party, he would stand up all of a sudden, much to Daisy's horror and dismay, and announce, "Now, before you all leave, I think we should have a word of prayer." No one up to that point had even thought of leaving. If they sat down again, he would go to the hall closet and bring someone's coat out. He would hold it up for all to see and ask, "Whose coat is this?" By that time they usually got the hint.

Oswald was never interested in sports, entertainment, or anything that did not pertain to his all-consuming work—getting the gospel out by preaching, writing books and poetry, and visiting the mission fields. This was his world! Daisy enabled him to remain in this almost unearthly world by taking more of the responsibility for home and children than did the average wife. Combined with his daily walk and communion with God, this was the secret of a great part of his unusual success.

Many people did not realize that Oswald was so otherworldly. One Sunday morning a lady approached him at church and exclaimed in great consternation, "I am surprised at you, Dr. Smith, allowing Hope to get her long hair cut. I don't think a Christian should have bobbed hair." He expressed his surprise at this, and when he arrived home, asked Hope to turn around. He wanted to have a look at her hair. Her hair had been short for some weeks but this was the first he realized it even though he had seen her every day.

On another occasion he was shaking hands with a long line of young people at the close of the service. Hope decided to get in the line to see if he would recognize her. Just as she thought, he gave her a hearty handshake and invited her back to the church. "I wonder if Dad ever feels the earth beneath his feet," she thought as she lay in bed that night thinking about him. "I wonder what it is like to live so close to God that everything about you seems so unimportant and trivial." All of his children loved him dearly and felt he was a person set apart, different from other fathers. But they knew that he, like Enoch of old, walked with God. Never a morning or evening passed that they did not hear his footsteps pacing up and down his room as he prayed.

At last the war ended and the children came back to Toronto once more. Hope, now settled after traveling a great deal during the past three years, much to Daisy's joy, presented her with her first grandchild, Peter. Daisy won his heart from the time he was a very small boy. She took him home for dinner every Sunday after church, and he always called her "Dais," as did all the rest of her grandchildren in the future.

Glen married Kay Powers, a lovely Christian girl whom he met at the church—the only girl he ever loved. She was one of the first seven young people to join the Sunday school of The Peoples Church. Soon after their little girl June was born, they moved away to Vancouver where Daisy had taken Glen as a child while Oswald was working amongst the lumberjacks of British Columbia. It was in Vancouver that Glen and Kay's two boys, Bruce and Christopher, were born.

Paul was assisting his father at the church then, and doing a lot of evangelistic work as well. He surprised his parents one day by introducing them to a little Irish girl, Anita Lawson, whom he married three months later. She was a great help to him in his meetings because she had a beautiful soprano voice and a sweet, winsome personality. She sang solos and duets with him as they traveled on campaigns all over Canada and the United States. They later had three children. They called their son Oswald Glen after his grandfather. After Glen was born Anita accompanied Paul to the Orient where she won the hearts of the people as she had learned to sing some of Oswald's songs in their language. Then God gave them two beautiful little girls, Jann and Jill.

A few years later Hope had another child, a little girl, Pauline, and later another boy, Paul James, named after her brother Paul. Daisy now had nine grandchildren, and Chrissie delighted in each one as she had loved their parents when they were children. Though she was a grandmother, Daisy still had a fascinating and busy life. She spoke frequently at banquets and luncheons, bringing helpful messages to women from her wealth of experience alongside her husband in the ministry.

One Monday morning as she was deciding on an appropriate text for her meeting that day, she was directed to Philippians 3:8—"... I have suffered the loss of all things..."—not knowing then that God was preparing her for the news that was to follow on her return from the meeting that day.

As she walked into her house after a wonderful time of blessing and fellowship with the women she heard the phone ringing and hastened to answer it. It was her brother Cress. He did not sound like his usual self, but, speaking in an anxious manner, he said, "I was talking to Mother on the phone, Daisy, and suddenly she stopped answering me. I knew something was wrong and I rushed over to the house and found her lying unconscious on the floor. The receiver was still dangling from the hook. I am with her now and the doctor is in the room checking her."

"Oh, Cress, not Mother! I will come immediately," she cried. Without removing her coat, Daisy ran back to the car and drove hurriedly through the traffic while her mind was flooded with thoughts of her dear mother. It was her mother who had introduced her to Jesus when she was just a little girl. She was not only her mother, but her dearest and best friend. She had been such a comfort to her when Oswald was often so far away. Then her text, "I have suffered the loss of all things," flashed into her mind. She felt instinctively that she was about to suffer the loss of her dearest friend on earth, her mother. "No love could ever be quite like Mother's love has been," she thought. She could not picture life without her. "Oh, God," she prayed aloud, "I have just been talking about suffering the loss of all things. Am I going to have to suffer such a great loss?"

Reaching the house, she flew in to find Cress waiting for her. She knew as soon as she looked at his pale face and solemn expression that her mother's condition must be serious. As they embraced each other, their tears mingled in silence and Daisy made her way to her mother's bedside. By this time, Ruth had returned from work and was sitting beside her, sobbing her heart out. She had never married, and had lived these many years with her mother, who was lying in a coma, unable to speak or see them. Daisy drew near, and taking her mother's hand in her own said softly, "Mother, it is Daisy. If you know I am here squeeze my hand." In a few seconds she felt a gentle, but assuring pressure. With tears flowing uncontrollably, she thanked God that though her mother could not speak or see, she knew Daisy was close beside her, and though Daisy could not see her heavenly Father, or hear His voice, she knew the room was filled with His presence.

Daisy thought of the many times her mother had been near her to reassure her from the time she was a little girl walking through the deep snow in Peterborough, huddled close to her mother's side. Daisy recalled how she had, in her childish way, offered to protect her mother beneath Jesus' cloak that she felt was covering her as they made their way to church facing the biting winds of winter, blowing and swirling in gusts before them.

She thought of the encouraging letters her mother had written to her during her years at Bible school and of how she had faithfully supported and prayed for her when she was working amongst the mountaineers in West Virginia. Her mother was always near to help her with her many problems and comfort her in her loneliness. As Daisy reflected on the past, she bowed her head and thanked God for giving her such a sweet, godly mother. With one arm around Ruth and the other around Cress, she looked up to God and simply prayed, "Thy will be done."

The doctor, who had been silently waiting to tell them that he did not expect Mrs. Billings to become conscious again, was deeply touched to hear Daisy pray, accepting whatever was God's will. Ten trying days followed as Ruth, Don, Cress, Violet, and Daisy took turns by the bedside, until at last God in His mercy gathered their precious mother up in His arms and took her to be with Himself.

Daisy's mother had said that when she died, she did not want her body laid out in a funeral parlor. To comply with her every wish, Daisy had the coffin placed in her living room until the time of the funeral. Her mother felt that the body, even though it is only the house in which the spirit dwells, is all that is left of the loved one, and to place it in a strange place is cold and callous and, she thought, unfeeling on the part of those who had suffered the loss. Daisy remembered that her mother had kept her father's body at home when he died many years before. This was to Daisy a rather strange wish, but it was her mother's request. As her brothers and sisters gathered for the funeral they did not sorrow as do those who do not know Christ, but rejoiced that though the body was in the room, their mother was with the Lord.

Oswald expressed his feelings best in the form of poetry and many times his poems brought great comfort to Daisy in times of distress. In tender, compassionate tones he read at the funeral a poem that he had written in memory of Daisy's mother, who had been a great inspiration to him:

Our Mother

Gone, gone at last, our one and only mother,
Gone to a world where none can ever die;
Sorrow and pain have left us brokenhearted,
Vainly we grope and ask the question, "Why?"

141

Why did she go? Her help was sorely needed,
  Courage and strength were ever hers to give;
How she enjoyed her final Sunday with us!
  Now she is gone who taught us how to live.

None ever heard her voice in public places,
  It was in secret that her work was done;
Yet how she loved the church and all its people!
  Filled was her heart with praise to God's dear Son.

O Mother dear, how quickly you departed!
  O how we'll miss your ever welcome smile!
God give us grace to bear the separation
  Until at last we bridge life's little while.

(From *Poems of a Lifetime*, p. 51.)

Part Two

8

Bound for South Africa

Sparkling white snow was gently falling in jewel-like flakes outside the window of 46 Buckingham Avenue, where Daisy and Oswald had been living for some time now. Though it was bright and sunny without, Daisy felt rather bleak and forlorn within. As she sat by the window knitting for her grandson, Peter, she was filled with nostalgia. She realized she would no longer be able to drop in and visit with her beloved mother for afternoon tea and be inspired by her composed spirit and beautiful Christian life. How she was going to miss her! She looked down at the tiny jacket she was knitting and thought about her three children, all married and away from her care forever.

Suddenly, she heard the car coming at great speed into the driveway. The car door slammed shut quickly. Looking out she saw her husband taking his usual long, fast, enthusiastic strides through the snow. The doorbell kept ringing until she had finished marking her place on her knitting pattern, put down her work, and opened the door. Oswald always rang the bell impatiently until he got some response.

Excitedly, without removing his rubbers or coat, he handed her a letter. "What do you think of that?" he exclaimed, before she had time to read it. While he was hanging up his coat, she took her place in her chair by the large bay window and began reading.

"Isn't that wonderful, Daisy, an invitation to visit South Africa?"

"Oh!" she cried, feeling less needed than ever, "Africa is so far away! It is a wonderful opportunity, but I wish you did not have to go such a great distance alone."

"I don't have to go alone," answered Oswald still jubilant.

"What do you mean? Are you going to take Paul with you?"

"No," he responded, with a mischievous sparkle in his blue eyes. "This time I am taking the best lady preacher that I know. I took her job from her at Dale Presbyterian Church, much to her disgust and dismay many years ago, and now I am going to let her voice be heard across the seas."

This seemed like an impossible dream come true. Jumping up from her chair Daisy exclaimed, "Are you sure they want me to go?"

"Of course they want you, but equally as important, I need you, and have waited a long time for you to be free to come with me," he assured her as he drew her into his arms and kissed her tenderly on the forehead. "You always said your place was with the children until they left home. You have stayed by them and now you are free to help me in my foreign work. Up until now I have been able to take you only on those rather short trips to Jamaica, Mexico, and Great Britain, but now with the children gone, we can embark on a major missionary venture to Africa—and stay for five months!"

It was a long sleepless night for Daisy as her heart throbbed with joy and her spirit ignited with excitement at the thought of a journey to a mystic, faraway land where she would see in action the missionaries for whom she had prayed.

Time slipped by swiftly after that night, and Daisy soon found herself standing alongside her husband, as if in a dream, before the great congregation of The Peoples Church who had come to bid them farewell. As she responded to the assurance of their prayers for divine protection, she quoted one of her favorite verses, Psalm 121:8—"The Lord shall preserve thy going out and thy coming in from this time forth, and even for evermore."

Two nights and a day and still the Pan American clipper soared across the ocean on its seemingly infinite journey. Since it was a sleepless night for Daisy, she traced the flight on her map as they winged over the endless expanse of the sands of the great Sahara Desert, stretching forever beneath them. From Dakar to Robertsfield, Liberia, and from there to Accra and the Gold Coast. From Accra over the great Congo River to Leopoldville in the Belgian Congo.

As Daisy stepped from the plane she could scarcely believe she was walking on African soil. Filled with curiosity, she glanced around the deserted-looking airport, then turned to Oswald and asked, "How will anyone know who we are?" Just then they noticed their names printed in large block letters on a square of cardboard fastened to a stick held high in the air by a single native. His husky voice boomed out, "Welcome, welcome!" Dropping the sign he bent low to clasp their hands in his. In this warm greeting they felt the love and gratitude of a man who was there to meet them because he had been converted by missionaries sent from their church some fourteen years before.

"I am Joshua Nbulu. My land-rover is waiting to take you to our mission station," he announced with a sparkle in his eyes and a broad, radiant smile. Unlike the smooth flight, the journey of this unique vehicle was extremely bumpy as they jostled from side to side over the many potholes and deep puddles along the way. They were staggered when Joshua told them of the ancestor and spirit worship in this country. "I doubt if there are more than a few families here who do not believe in the spirits and witchcraft," he declared.

As they approached the village it was a moving experience for them to hear in the distance the harmonious voices of an African choir singing in their typical rhythmic way the song, "He Lives." Their happy faces testified to the fact that God was alive and all their false gods had been renounced. They were out in great throngs to welcome them.

As Oswald walked toward them, one of the African choir members marveled that he was actually going to meet the author of the book entitled *The Salvation of God*. This book had led him to believe in the only God. As Oswald looked over the shoulder of this humble African, still grasping his hand in gratitude, he noticed that Daisy had not taken long to discover two of their own missionaries. Excitedly she brought them to greet her husband. "Oswald, look who are here, Don and Florence who sang in our choir so long ago. Who would have thought they would be conducting a choir of their own in Africa!" Oswald stepped forward to grip their hands with his usual enthusiastic handshake, when Don interrupted him by saying, "We would not be here if it had not been for the vision received at one of your missionary conventions."

"It is one thing to see the need, Don, but the important thing is to be obedient in carrying out the commission of Christ, as you have both done so faithfully," replied Oswald.

Following this warm welcome, Oswald spent four strenuous days ministering in the village. He, along with Daisy, was touched and stirred by the insatiable hunger the people showed for God's Word as each service lasted anywhere from two to four hours.

Five days had slipped by swiftly, when Joshua reluctantly loaded their bags on his land-rover. Before leaving, Daisy, still deeply moved by all she had seen, felt constrained to speak a few words of encouragement and farewell. Turning to Joshua, she asked, "Would you interpret for me?" He readily responded, but being concerned about her small stature, and anxious that all should see and hear her, he proudly helped her onto a nearby ant hill, the most unique platform from which she had ever spoken! Later, Joshua, taken with her warmth and sincerity, and almost blinded by tears of appreciation, drove his esteemed ambassadors for Christ to the nearest airstrip where he reluctantly parted with them, as he felt he might never see them again.

Upon boarding the single-engine plane, with room for only two passengers, Daisy asked the ever confident Oswald, "Are you sure this plane will get us to our destination?" Her apprehension and insecurity mounted as she peered out the tiny window, and with the sound of the motor thundering in her ears saw Joshua smile and point to the skies, indicating he would see them above if not on this earth again! To her relief the plane made a safe take-off for Rhodesia.

As soon as they had fastened their seat belts and begun to feel more composed, the pilot suddenly looked at them with a distressed expression on his face, and pleaded, "If you have ever prayed hard, pray harder now. I am afraid we are out of petrol." At this point suddenly the plane appeared to make a nose dive. Daisy looking frantically to the earth below felt it was rising up to meet her. She spontaneously cried to God for help. Presently, the pilot's intense expression changed as he announced, "Everything is all right. I have just switched the other tank on and there is some petrol left in it." With that, the little plane zoomed up into the deep blue African sky, and after considerable hill-hopping, eventually landed in Rhodesia.

This was a memorable part of the journey as it included the famous Victoria Falls so aptly described by the Africans as "The Smoke That Thunders," its massive spray soaring one hundred feet into the air. These waterfalls are one and a quarter miles wide and four hundred feet high. Few Christians visiting the falls, one of the seven wonders of the world, do so without thinking of the wonder God wrought through the life of David Livingstone, the explorer and missionary who fought his way through fever-infested jungles in the midst of sav-age tribes, and discovered the falls in 1855. He died on his knees, praying for his beloved African people. The natives took nine months to carry his body fifteen hundred miles on a toilsome and perilous road to the coast to be shipped to England and buried in Westminster Abbey. Significantly, his heart was buried on the shores of the Zambesi River, beneath a tree on which they carved his name.

Ministering together in Rhodesia, Oswald and Daisy witnessed scenes surpassing all they had surveyed at the falls, for the events that followed were of eternal value. During their services in Salisbury hundreds of people responded to their invitations, dedicating their lives to missionary work, while many more accepted Christ as Lord and Savior. Oswald was inspired anew, as he recalled the indomitable courage and vision of Livingstone who had left a trail of light, traveling thirty thousand miles through the heart of Africa. Oswald realized that if Livingstone had not pioneered Christianity in the heart of the African jungle, such results would not be theirs today.

After holding meetings in Salisbury, and several other major cities of Rhodesia, they continued on to Pretoria, the administrative capital and seat of the civil service of South Africa. They were met by Mr. and Mrs. von Staden. Mr. von Staden, founder and director of the Dorothea Mission, possessed a transcending, burning religious fervor which animated his whole being and every act. After an exchange of greetings over afternoon tea, served so graciously in their home, Mr. von Staden leaned forward and discussed with great enthusiasm the energetic itinerary he had planned for them for the following three weeks.

No time was lost, as that evening they found themselves approaching one of the famous Dutch Reformed Churches where it had been advertised Oswald would speak. Daisy, much to her surprise, was also expected to bring greetings. As she ascended the long flight of steps leading to the beautiful hand-carved mahogany pulpit and canopy, characteristic of the Dutch Reformed Church, her mind flashed back to the sharp contrast of the humble little platform from which she had spoken only days before in the African mission station. This memory inspired her to bring an effective appeal and share the burden of the needs she had so recently seen.

The next morning, just before leaving for the Alexandra location where ninety thousand natives lived, Mr. von Staden walked into the room and turning to Oswald with an amused expression on his face, said, "You have already made headlines in the Pretoria newspaper!" A quotation from the article read, "Dressed in a habit, this tall, lean, white-haired Canadian looked like a Medieval Monk, but the resemblance is only superficial. Out of the pulpit he is friendly and genial."

Oswald and Daisy, still chuckling over this accurate description, picked up their suitcase and walked towards the car.

It was a scenic drive for Daisy especially as they made their way through avenues of jacoranda trees in full bloom, spreading a carpet of her favorite color, petals of lavender on either side.

The scene changed dramatically for her, however, when, shortly after, the vast Alexandra location came into view. The outcome of one man's singular dedication soon became apparent as they drove many miles through this vast mission field for which their friend had poured out his life in untiring effort to bring the message of true freedom through Christ.

Mr. von Staden stopped alongside a simple, humble dwelling where he had arranged for them to have lunch

152

with one of his native pastors. Though delighted to meet Oswald and Daisy, Jeremy, the pastor, was obviously proud of his spiritual white father. Turning to them and then pointing in the distance, he said, with deep emotion, "As far as your eyes can see, all around you, Mr. von Staden's voice and message of hope have been heard by our people here."

"It is evident from all we have seen and heard this morning that God has given to you a great leader," replied Oswald.

Mr. von Staden modestly interrupted, "I think it is time for you to have something to eat."

"What about you, Mr. von Staden?" asked Daisy. "You must be hungry. You had so little for breakfast."

"I'm not particularly hungry," he replied. "I eat very little." Food seemed to be so unimportant to this man, thought Daisy, as she sized him up in her mind, journeying back to the rondovel where they were to spend the night. But there was no question of his appetite for the things of God. He was such a quiet, unassuming, frail-looking man, and yet obviously a spiritual giant.

As the darkness fell, Daisy and Oswald said goodnight to him and asked him to assure Jeremy of their appreciation and prayers since they would not see him again before leaving for the Kruger National Park the next day.

Securing the net provided to keep insects away, Daisy said, "I wish the mountaineers of West Virginia had thought of something like this!" Looking around, she examined her new primitive surroundings—thatched roof above, and walls of clay supporting it.

"One thing about this place, Oswald," she said, "they wouldn't have much housework to do, would they?

I wonder what the women do with all their spare time," she continued, little knowing at that point how very hard many African women work in other ways. Adjusting to her strange new environment she began to settle down for the night and reflect on the day and their trip thus far. She thought of the inspiration her husband's hymns and books had brought to this mission station as well as to the others she had visited, and with a warm glow in her heart, knowing he belonged to her, fell asleep.

Early the next morning the von Stadens picked them up and set out for the reserve.

"Every day holds fascinating unexpected joys as we continue this trip. I have been looking forward with great anticipation to seeing this famous game reserve," remarked Daisy to Mrs. von Staden.

"Did you know," she replied, "it is five hundred miles long and fifty miles wide? It stands as a memorial to Paul Kruger, who at one time was the president of this country, and a great lover of animals and birds." All of this added to Daisy's interest as they drove from Pretoria through fertile farming country, and the low veld of the Transvaal, on up the mountains, then descending to the valleys amidst lush fruit lands. They were anxious to arrive at the gates of the park before six o'clock to register in one of the camps for the night. Otherwise they would be compelled to sleep in the car until the gates reopened at six in the morning or retrace their journey back to the nearest motel.

Excitement permeated the air as they entered the reserve in plenty of time to get a glimpse of some of Africa's wild animals in their natural environment. They had seen such animals only in a zoo behind wired cages, but as they drove along the dusty road Daisy said, with a chuckle, "I feel as if we are the ones in the zoo and the animals are scrutinizing us."

"Yes," laughed her friend, "we certainly are the ones in the cage. We dare not so much as roll down the windows."

Suddenly, they were almost breathless as they sighted a herd of zebras grazing near the roadside. "Look, Oswald," cried Daisy, "I have counted twenty-five of them so far. What beautiful markings they have!"

"And God has made each one different!" added Mrs. von Staden. Oswald, forgetting all the rules of the reserve, in his excitement quickly rolled down the car window and began taking movies of these unique animals. He wanted to show his congregation what seemed to be nature's playground.

They watched the springbok, impala, and gazelles, some feeding, others hopping across the road in long, graceful leaps—beautiful beyond description. The impala gazed at them with such soft, pleading eyes. Noticing the wart hogs Oswald asked, 'Should I take a shot of them?"

"No," replied Daisy emphatically, "they are far too ugly!"

"Oh," laughed Mrs. von Staden, "do you want your people to be impressed only by the handsome animals?"

"Don't roll down the window," screamed Daisy as a huge lion ambled up close to the car. But, down went the window, and Oswald's hand trembled with excitement as the massive head of the king of the beasts filled the lens of his camera.

Just beyond the lion, the African skyscraper, the giraffe, stalked about eating the leaves from the tall trees, his great long neck clearly outlined against the blue of the sky.

As they neared a river, with an armed native, they made their way to the water's edge where at least a dozen hippopotamuses were sprawled on a submerged sand bar, most of them asleep.

"Go and stand in front of them, Daisy," said Oswald. "I want to show the people at home how close you were to the hippos." Daisy, smitten with fear, reluctantly placed herself where he wanted her. Just as he was ready to take the picture, one of the hippos gave a gaping yawn, and at that moment she knew for the first time how Jonah must have felt!

Oswald was always a lover of birds. At one time he had a huge cage in his own room at home with all kinds of birds, including seventeen budgies of various colors. He was spellbound watching these birds in their great array of color swooping overhead as they entered the camp just at dusk.

Retiring to their respective rondovels, Oswald turned to Daisy with a twinkle in his eye, and said, "It isn't every night we are serenaded to sleep by the haunting sounds of a mixed chorus of wild beasts!"

"True," replied Daisy, as she snuggled into her covers securely. "They can serenade us all night as long as they stay outside this camp!" As if that were not enough to keep one awake, momentarily, Oswald's loud snoring joined the chorus. For them it had been a night to remember in the midst of a completely new world!

A new day dawned which found the von Stadens waiting to escort them to their car which had already joined the long line of cars eagerly waiting for the Sukuza Park gates to open at six for another day's adventure. As they crept silently along the gravel road, they suddenly caught sight of a leopard on a rock five yards away. This magnificently spotted animal had the power within him to destroy the innocent little impala grazing nearby. Instinctively aware of the impending danger, this harmless, agile creature glanced nervously about him, gripped by the constant fear of being devoured. He leapt at least seven feet into the air, fleeing for refuge.

Later they were awed by the sight of lions having a noonday feast, consisting of a giraffe sprawled across the veld. Greedy vultures swooped down waiting their turn to pick up the leftovers. "What destruction!" exclaimed Daisy. Forcefully, a truth gripped her heart, and turning to Mrs. von Staden, she asked, "Isn't it incredible that even here in an area where the beasts of the field seem free and uninhibited they are bound under God's curse as much as are all mankind?" Sobering thoughts subdued Daisy and caused her to withdraw from those about her, as they made their way out of the Kruger Park that day. Her first impressions of this animal kingdom had led her to believe that here was a place where God's creatures were born free. They were free to roam, to explore, to enjoy their surroundings. Apparently there were no such things here as greed, destruction, tension, and insecurity. This was the perfect environment intended by God for mankind from the beginning of time. However, after all she had seen she concluded that amidst nature's land of apparent freedom, even these magnificent creatures were beset by the same curse that was destroying civilization. This curse

God had pronounced on all His creation from the beginning because man chose to disobey His laws rather than enjoy the perfect environment created for him.

As she watched the warm colors of the tropical sun setting, she thought of the New Day that would dawn eternally when God's promise of a new heaven and earth would replace this bondage forever. The New Day would usher in an age of harmony and peace—"The wolf also shall dwell with the lamb, and the leopard shall lie down with the kid; and the calf and the young lion and the fatling together; and a little child shall lead them" (Isaiah 11:6).

Enroute to Kimberly they observed with intense interest primitive native life. Daisy, impressed by the vastly different cultural background of the people, turned to her traveling companion and expressed her astonishment at the stark contrast between the hard lot of a woman in Africa and the affluence of Canadians. These women were laden down with huge beads they had strung together and wound around their necks and ankles. They wore heavy brass rings on their arms. To Daisy it seemed symbolic of hardships endured and burdens borne by a race so long bound by superstition, struggling for survival. Children were naked and the women had very little clothing. Their faces were painted with yellow ocher to protect them from the hot tropical sun. The thatched huts were fragile and insecure. More desperate than their poverty-stricken condition, however, was their spiritual impoverishment concerning the things of God.

"You see, Mrs. Smith," explained her friend, "women here are still victims of an ancient pagan custom.

They can be purchased from their fathers in exchange for the number of cattle their admirers can afford. To pay this bride-price they think nothing of stealing the white man's beasts. Theft to them is a manly sport and not considered dishonorable unless the thief is discovered. Though Daisy's reaction was one of horror, it was also one of humor as she commented, "I wonder how many cows it would take to buy us."

"Far more than our husbands could ever afford," Mrs. von Staden rejoined with a smile.

Daisy further observed the unbelievable bundles of firewood these women carried on their heads. Others, with backs bent in the heat of the sun, were cutting sugar cane. The African men were lying down, lazily smoking their pipes. "What a difference from women of the western world," she thought, "where the introduction of Christianity first liberated them from such slavery!" The look of despair and sadness on their faces haunted Daisy day and night. The spiritual impact of her experiences on this trip was to be revolutionary. She turned to Mr. von Staden, and said, thoughtfully, "After what I have seen today, and at your mission station, I will never be the same. I know I will return home to present the cause of missions with a grasp of its need and a compassion that hitherto have been only theory." She had a new understanding now of her husband's burning vision that continually compelled him to go to the ends of the earth.

Oswald approached his wife the following day and asked, "How would you like to go down into a diamond mine? Mr. von Staden tells me that South Africa produces more gem diamonds than any other country and that their value is nearly half that of all gem diamonds marketed throughout the world. These famous diamond mines are near here in Kimberly, and they would like to take us to see them."

"Diamonds!" exclaimed Daisy, "bordering such poverty?" Then, glancing down at the tiny diamond Oswald had placed on her finger that magic night on the Humber River, she could scarcely believe she was about to see a real diamond mine.

Looking wistfully at him, though knowing full well what the answer would be, she questioned, "Is it your intention to add a couple of diamonds to my little ring?" Before he could answer, she prepared to leave.

When they reached the mines they donned a pair of overalls and proceeded on an elevator to the bowels of the earth. As they descended, Daisy thought of how hard miners worked to cut through rugged rock to find these precious stones just as we must search into God's Word to come up with gems of truth. On emerging from the mine, as the men wandered back toward the car, Daisy and her friend lingered, looking at the precious jewels on display. By now they had formed a deep bond of friendship in which Daisy felt free to express her innermost thoughts.

Unconstrained, she began to think aloud as she said, "Nothing of any real value comes easily." She recalled the story of the most valuable diamond in history, the gigantic Cullinan diamond discovered in an African mine and presented to the English monarch, King Edward VII, in 1907 by the government of the Transvaal in South Africa. Before it could be used in the head of the scepter it had to be sent to an expert lapidary. With a solid blow he split the priceless jewel in four pieces. That blow was no mistake. It had been carefully planned. It resulted in bringing the gem to its most brilliant and jeweled splendor. "Our Creator, the most skilled lapidary, never makes a mistake," she said thoughtfully. "Sometimes our nerves wince and our hearts are broken at the stinging blows that crush our lives, causing us to question His dealings with us. Too often we forget that in His eyes we are His most priceless jewels. Every blow He permits to fall upon us is working out our spiritual enrichment. Though we may not see the reason for these blows at the time, they are necessary to make us of value to Him."

Turning to Mrs. von Staden she said, "The diamonds we held were worth thousands of dollars. Those valuable stones sent out light, brilliant light in every direction, whichever way they were turned. How much they resemble a true Christian, transformed by the Master's touch! This should make us want more than ever to let the light of our lives sparkle and shine as we in turn touch other lives."

Mrs. von Staden, who had been listening intently to Daisy, squeezed her arm in her irresistibly warm way, and deeply moved, said, "Do you realize you have just given me enough material to pass on to my husband for his sermon next Sunday? I wish I had time to listen to you a little longer, but the men are already in the car waiting for us to leave for the airport." Reluctantly, they hurried to join their husbands.

The moment for parting had come and feelings of admiration, friendship and deep gratitude were expressed to the von Stadens for all they had done. As the plane took off for Capetown, Daisy and Oswald watched their friends waving good-bye until they disappeared from view. As they settled down in their seats they felt they had parted with two truly great friends.

Capetown, the southernmost point of this vast continent, the mother city of South Africa, is also the legislative capital and the seat of Parliament. It not only holds the key to the Indian and Atlantic Oceans but unlocks the door to the history of this country with its vastly different cultural backgrounds.

The only indigenous people with whom the early white settlers came into contact were the nomadic Hottentots and Bushmen. The latter have remained a separate people living in the semidesert areas of the Northwestern Cape and neighboring territories where they continue their stone-age existence. The Hottentots were decimated by two epidemics of smallpox. After the arrival of the Dutch settlers, those who survived intermarried with other races over the years. Their descendants constitute the main body of what today are called the "Cape Colored." The white people of Capetown have a sophisticated life-style which resembles the fashion-conscious, cultural and artistic ways of Paris.

The Bantu, known as the black people, consist of several distinct nations. Primarily of mixed Negroid descent, each with their own customs and traditions, these nations migrated southward. After the frontier wars of the eighteenth and nineteenth century, the whites and blacks in many cases returned to the old Bantu homelands.

The old and new homesteads clearly characterize the many facets of the South African scene. The ultramodern design of present-day British and European architecture contrasts sharply with the gaily-painted mud huts which appear as if from nowhere, either near large cities or in the vast expanses of veld in the countryside.

Daisy and Oswald were met by Mr. A. J. A. Rowlands, a patriarch of the Christian faith, known to many for his cordiality and genuine interest in strangers. This was no ordinary reception, since here was a man who for decades had been famous for his unique ministry of welcoming Christian workers from overseas, whether it meant a trip to the harbor, train station or airport. As he stooped over to grip their hands with a firm handshake, the deep lines in his face and his furrowed brow clearly revealed that this dear saint was well over ninety years of age. Their greetings were suddenly interrupted by the contagious, enthusiastic welcome of Rev. Glyn Tudor, Oswald's friend of long standing and co-ordinator of his meetings. Together they pressed their way through the crowded airport to Mr. Tudor's car to glimpse the beautiful city of Capetown.

As Mr. Tudor drove them, they felt they were moving through a world of flora. There were twenty thousand species of wild flowers, the richest variety in the world. The Cape Province was unequaled for its exotic plants and flowering trees. The opulent white-gabled houses harmonized perfectly with the surrounding majestic mountain ranges. Monuments to the early white settlers shaped the landscape and soon made the Smiths aware of the intriguing history of this nation. It was apparent to them that locked into the mind of every adult was a childhood memory of those difficult pioneering days when the Dutch, British, German and French struggled for white supremacy.

The Dutch Reformed Church has been the strongest denomination in South Africa, its members forming the most powerful element of the government. Probably the most famous among their numerous churches is the

Groote Kirk (the mother church), where Rev. Andrew Murray had ministered, and where the Smiths were scheduled to speak.

Ministering in this historic place was a highlight for Daisy particularly, since Andrew Murray was one of her favorite authors and preachers. They also paid a visit to his church in Wellington. As they approached this imposing white edifice, they were thrilled by the sight of a life-size white stone statue of Andrew Murray adorning the front of the church as a monument in memory of him. The spiritual emphasis of his ministry had made a lasting impact upon this denomination in South Africa, and his influence was felt throughout all the churches.

The following day, Mrs. Tudor took Daisy to the Cape Colored Township, a short distance by car from Capetown's affluent culture, to speak at a mass meeting for colored women only. Her heart was moved with deep compassion for these people as she realized they were not recognized as being either black or white, the result of intermarriage decades ago, and therefore rejected by society. The colored in Capetown lived in homes with cracked plaster and crumbling, broken windows, rough wooden floors and the sound of rats running all over. While the majority lived in pitiful conditions in those days there were some who lived in finer homes as they do today.

Daisy experienced an exceptionally warm glow in her heart as she proclaimed Christ's message of freedom to all races and the glorious fact that whoever receives Him will be accepted into the family of God. That night Oswald preached to the Colored in the football stadium. There was an overflow crowd of six thousand present. Many sat on the ground and listened, so great was their hunger to know more of God.

A thrilling moment of their visit through this province occurred when Mr. Rowlands took them by cable car to the top of Capetown's famous Table Mountain. As they surveyed the magnificent grandeur and rugged beauty of the Cape, Daisy, silently wishing everyone she knew could share this moment with her, and feeling so minute, turned to Oswald and said, "Amidst such splendor, my mind can think only of the third and fourth verses of Psalm 8—'When I consider thy heavens, the work of thy fingers, the moon and the stars, which thou hast ordained; What is man, that thou art mindful of him? and the son of man, that thou visitest him?'"

Although they were booked to fly from Capetown to Durban, new-found friends, Mr. and Mrs. Ferguson, generously offered to drive them over a thousand miles via the scenic Garden Route of the Cape, through the tribal land of the Transkei. This part of the country had few trees, vast rolling hills and plains. They passed many of the "red blanket people"of the Xhosa tribe. The features of these people were more Arabic than Negroid. The men, tall and well-built, raised cattle. They preserved their ancient traditions and intricate clan systems, and they had their own royalty. Though they were fierce fighters they were equally gifted poets. In spite of the tropical sun, they were wrapped in colorful heavy blankets. Riding on horseback they covered long stretches of semidesert and shrubland. Thousands of sheep grazed on their plains.

"Would you believe, Dr. Smith," said Mr. Ferguson, "that the witch doctors used to smell out their victims, and then hurl them over steep precipices to their death, or cover them with oil, bind them and lay them beside ant hills to be eaten alive by the ants—a terrible death! They also used to drive sharp wooden stakes into the bodies of their victims," he continued, "leaving them to die in indescribable agony."

"Do they still do that?" asked Daisy, cringing at the thought of such gruesome behavior.

"Many of these extreme practices were done away with by the South African government; they became totally nonexistent when the gospel of Christ was introduced, but superstition still prevails among the majority of the Xhosa people."

Oswald, equally disturbed by these atrocities, said with deep, willful conviction and in strong, deliberate tones, "To think that so many in our country are keeping to themselves the knowledge of Christ and the freedom He gives, while these people live and die in ignorance. The last command Christ gave us was to go into all the world and preach the gospel. We must find a way to help the missionaries who, along with the Dutch Reformed Church, are doing everything they can to evangelize these people, even if it takes all our time and effort for the rest of our lives!"

Perhaps the most moving experience of the journey for Daisy was the sight of scores of African children trailing their little car as it wound its way slowly through the hills on the dizzy roads. The Transkei villages, unlike others they had seen, were unique in that their white-walled homes were artistically painted in a variety of colorful designs. Some of the women were seated in front of their homes and smoking long pipes, while others were doing their work with babies asleep on their backs. As Mr. Ferguson slowed down for Oswald to photograph them, Daisy decided to scatter a number of tracts out the window. These tracts were a translation into their language of Oswald's "Only One Way." She could never forget the expression on the faces of those who scrambled furiously in the dust to get their hands on a copy. Eagerly scanning the message, they passed it on to their friends, only to run back frantically to grasp for more.

"I have never seen good news travel so fast," said Daisy. "They seem to be coming from every direction. Look at them, Oswald, pressing their way to the car, and now I have no more tracts to give," she sighed with a heavy heart. She thought of the indifference and apathy of so many back home who took for granted the unparalleled opportunities that were theirs through constant exposure to God's Word.

Seated at the dinner table in the Umtata Hotel where they were to spend the night, Daisy, still deeply impressed with what she had seen that day, struggled through her meal. As she recalled the spiritual hunger and hopeless expressions portrayed on the faces of that tribe, she put down her knife and fork and said, emphatically, "The more I see of missionary work, the more I feel that although education is necessary, it is not the answer to their basic longings. Our job is to give them the gospel. It is the only power that can liberate them from such deep-seated superstition and fear."

As they prepared to retire that night, Oswald walked out onto a little balcony adjoining their room. Daisy's profound words, combined with all he had seen and heard that day, completely absorbed his thoughts. She wondered why he was so quiet and what was detaining him. She was almost asleep when he returned, and recited to her the words of a poem God had just given him—"Give

Them the Gospel." Only after he had unburdened his heart by writing the following additional verses was he able to settle down to sleep:

> Give them, Oh, give them the Gospel;
>   Why should they die in their sin?
> Tell them, Oh, tell them of Jesus;
>   They are so burdened within.
>
> Long have they waited in darkness,
>   Waited for someone to go;
> Long have they sought in their blindness,
>   Jesus the Savior to know.

That poem, set to music later, proved to be a real challenge and blessing at their missionary conventions ever after.

There was a noticeable drop in altitude as they continued their journey amidst flowing hills and a profusion of flowers and vegetation down towards sea level to the beautiful city of Durban on the Indian Ocean. At the time this was South Africa's largest port and second largest on the continent.

After they parted with their traveling companions, they were immediately taken into the home of Jack and Alec Rowlands, who were the ministers in charge of what could be considered the largest work amongst the Indian people of South Africa. Much to Daisy's surprise, she discovered that these two middle-aged ministers were brothers who had never married, but had given their undivided attention and time to the spiritual welfare of the East Indians in that city and surrounding districts. These people first migrated to South Africa in 1860 as indentured laborers on the sugar plantations in the Province of Natal under an arrangement sponsored by the British government. Their numbers increased as traders, merchants and craftsmen, lawyers, doctors, brokers and industrialists, as well as semiskilled laborers migrated on their own initiative. They were predominantly Hindus and Muslims, their main languages being Tamil, Hindi, and Telegu.

As they drove through this modern city, it was incredible to see side by side with the African and white people this third race numbering in the thousands, a miniature India. A mosque stood opposite a Protestant cathedral; Indian women, a picture in their striking saris, intermingled with Europeans in modern apparel. African women primitively dressed outnumbered the Indians as they pushed and squeezed their way through the crowds, hoping to find a bargain at a nearby Indian market.

Suddenly Jack Rowlands pulled his car to the side of the road and said, "You are most fortunate indeed. You are about to witness a parade that is not an everyday occurrence in our city, but one which continues to take place as a sad and constant reminder of the bondage that still exists among these Indian people." Presently in the distance could be heard the eerie chanting sounds of fanatic Indian Muslims leading an unusual procession. These zealots had needles forced through their extended tongues; hooks from which hung pomegranates pierced their chests. Trailing behind them rattled old wooden carts carrying their gaudy, hideous, fearful-looking gods. As these gods were believed to be of no further use, they were being taken to the Umgene River to be buried. It was a custom to end such a day of ceremony with some of these Indians walking barefoot on hot coals of fire.

Starting up the car once more, Jack Rowlands spoke.

"You can understand better now why we have devoted our lives to giving the message of Christ's freedom to these people." As he related the story of thousands of Indians that had embraced Christianity, he drove on to show some of the Christian temples they had built. Daisy was eager to attend the service at Bethesda Temple, where she and Oswald had been asked to speak the following Sunday morning.

Sitting on the platform, she noticed that the women assembled on one side of the church and remained seated, while the men opposite them stood to pray. At the conclusion of the service many renounced their false gods and bowed down in acceptance of the only true God and Creator of all mankind.

For many years Jack Rowlands and his brother had been friends of Rev. and Mrs. John Wooderson, whose church had a substantial part in supporting this Indian work.

The following day the Wooderson family arranged to take Daisy and Oswald to see the ever growing work being carried on in the European and African churches. During the drive, Oswald was fascinated while photographing the famous Zulu war dances. He was also captivated by the colorful rickshaw boys with their lofty, massive, heavily beaded headdress. It was amusing to watch them spring unbelievably high into the air as they pulled their uneasy tourists, bouncing up and down behind them.

Finally they stopped for afternoon tea at Athlone Park, a picturesque setting overlooking the sea. It was a sunny afternoon as they relaxed beneath the flowering trees and were served by one of the Indian waiters. However, to Daisy's astonishment they had scarcely sat down when monkeys from everywhere, swinging on the branches overhead, leaped down to join them for tea! Daisy, squirming uneasily in her seat, and glancing quickly from side to side, exclaimed, "You would think we had just rung the dinner bell! How do they know tea is ready? It looks as if they have brought all their loved ones with them!"

Looking half-terrified at Mrs. Wooderson, she asked timidly, "Are you not afraid one of these creatures might bite you?"

"Oh, no," she replied, amused at Daisy's question. "We've lived here all our lives and never once have we been bitten," she assured her with the utmost confidence. Daisy, still feeling disturbed, tried to enjoy her tea when suddenly a monkey sprang forward and took a sizable piece out of Mrs. Wooderson's leg. Never had Daisy's feet carried her so swiftly as she deposited herself back safely in the car. After first-aid treatment was administered, they returned to the Woodersons' home to meet the rest of the family.

They were introduced to Norma Cooper, Mrs. Wooderson's youngest sister, an attractive ordained minister, who at that time was assisting her brother-in-law in the ministry. Norma expressed her gratitude to them for the service held in the Central Methodist Church where she had been deeply challenged by Oswald's message introducing the concept of a faith promise offering. As a direct result of this, she conducted the first missionary convention in their church. Until that time this church, like others, budgeted only a small percentage of their income to support missionaries. This new concept stirred not only the members of this church, but the entire organization in South Africa to conduct similar missionary conventions. Little did Oswald and Daisy realize the spark they had lit in Durban was to fan a flame of missionary zeal, the results of which only eternity would reveal.

While Daisy was packing for her departure to Johannesburg, her days of sunshine in Durban were suddenly clouded. Mrs. Wooderson entered the room, and with saddened eyes, in a quiet, subdued manner, said, "It is hard for me to be the bearer of such sad news, Mrs. Smith, but a cable has just been phoned through from Canada to say that your sister Violet has just passed away."

Daisy, slowly dropping the last dress into the case, found it difficult to hold back the tears, but in her usual composed way, with a thoughtful, distant look in her eyes, and a heart flooded with loving memories of her sister, expressed all of those things that had endeared Violet to her from their childhood years. "You know, Mrs. Wooderson," she began, "Violet in her youth was always carefree and frivolous, but as she matured she became more serious-minded and deeply interested in missions. Although she could not be a missionary, she gave generously to send others. When we parted, she told me that she might go to be with her Savior before I returned, but her last words to me were, 'My part will be to lie here and pray for you.' She felt that what I was doing was important, and she begged me not to remain at home because she was sick." Mrs. Wooderson listened with deep sympathy; then kneeling beside the bed, she placed her arm around Daisy and prayed for the comfort and peace only God could impart to her in the loss of her sister.

As the Wooderson family, joined by the Rowland brothers and their friends, waved good-bye, the plane soared high into the blue, leaving the rain and heavy clouds behind. The veil of mist lifted now in the brilliance of the sun. Daisy was reminded of the brightness of that eternal day that would break with the clarity of crystal. The clouds below resembled fields snowy with cotton that would some day part forever and she would be united with those she loved once more. As she stared out the window with tear-dimmed eyes, knowing that eternal life awaits every child of God, the comforting words of a song she had recently heard came to her saddened heart:

> Just think of stepping ashore and finding it Heaven,
> Of touching a hand and finding it God's,
> Of breathing new air and finding it celestial,
> Of waking in Glory and finding it Home.

In her distant thoughts she pictured all of her friends and relatives at Violet's funeral. Her thoughts were interrupted when Oswald took her hand, and in sympathetic tones said, "If it were not for devoted Christians like your sister, who feel their part in the Great Commission is to support missionaries and pray, many works for God such as we have just seen in Durban could never have been accomplished. God has given to everyone a responsibility toward others. Each of us will have to answer for himself that day when we see Him face to face."

A royal welcome awaited them in Johannesburg. A civic reception at the city hall had been arranged by Mayor L. V. Hurd. It consisted mainly of a group of ministers who had gathered for morning tea. Daisy soon felt at home as she discovered that Mrs. Hurd, sitting beside her at the head table, was a child of God.

An exciting day had been planned for them as Rev.

Gerald Ford, who had organized their meetings in that city, took them to the gold mines. They were astounded when he told them that 77 percent of the gold of the free world was produced in South Africa and that in terms of mineral wealth it is one of the richest countries in the world, mining more than fifty minerals.

They were quite a sketch, donned in overalls, boots, and helmet, as they stepped into a portable cage and descended nine thousand feet in pitch black darkness. "This reminds me," remarked Oswald, "of what the Bible calls 'the blackness of darkness.'" He was obviously thinking of eternal separation from God.

As the elevator doors opened, Daisy looked aghast at the two hundred and fifty steps she still had to descend to the depths of the mine. She was feeling overcome and stifled by this darkness and confinement. Just when she wondered what her prospects were of ever emerging from that abyss, Mr. Ford informed them that this was the very spot where the King of England had fainted when he visited the mine. Daisy, wide-eyed and trembling, reluctantly edged her way inch by inch into a still darker tunnel where they stooped, staggered by the sight of a solid brick of gold weighing seventy-five pounds and worth $35,000 at that time. Surrounding them was the constant activity of eleven thousand blacks working in the underground passages.

As they left the mine to prepare for the evening service, a deep and lasting impression had been indelibly imprinted on their hearts and minds. It was not so much the wealth of this area of concentrated riches, as the fact that this wealth could not buy the freedom millions of Africans were crying out for day after day. Nor could it solve the incredible variety of complex problems so long associated with that land. Lasting hope for their future in this life, or in the life to come, could not be purchased with mere gold. The price was paid two thousand years ago with the precious lifeblood of Christ, the sinless, spotless Lamb of God described in I Peter 1:18, 19. Mark 8:36 repeated itself over and over in Oswald's mind as he thought about a text for his sermon that night—"What shall it profit a man if he gain the whole world, and lose his own soul?" Through the combined ministry of Oswald and Daisy many discovered, not material possessions, but imperishable riches of peace and security in Christ.

The major crusades that Oswald had conducted in the country of South Africa during that visit were held in the large Dutch Reformed Churches, and to this day, many ministers in that great denomination thank God for the ministry of Oswald and Daisy because it marked the beginning of a new missionary emphasis throughout the Dutch Reformed Churches there.

After a royal send-off at the Jan Smuts International Airport, they departed for home via Rome, Paris, and London.

Though the journey was tiresome and seemed endless, Daisy knew in her heart that time and distance could never blot out the memories of the past three months. Leaning forward and looking intently into Oswald's deep blue eyes, she said sincerely, "Now I understand that one must see other parts of the world and the people there for himself if he is ever to fully understand the great need that exists in the unevangelized countries. I shall be forever grateful to you, Oswald, for making this trip possible," she added.

"We can both thank God for permitting us to be His ambassadors," he replied. Consenting to no further distraction, he continued to read the biography of David Livingstone. Daisy reclined with closed eyes and in her solitude she could understand why those who leave the shores of South Africa invariably return, for that land casts a spell on most people, seizing them in a passionate grip. But she felt clasped by a stronger hold—an awesome, unshakable responsibility never known before. As the Pan American silver eagle bore her speedily on towards her homeland, she prayed that God would enable her to transmit something of this burden to the women at home. She wanted them to understand the need more clearly so that they could pray effectively, knowing most of them had not had, and indeed would never have, the opportunity to visit Africa.

Shortly after their arrival in Toronto, Daisy's heart was warmed as she read a letter from her dear friends the von Stadens:

Dear Dr. and Mrs. Smith:

How empty South Africa feels without you! The morning you left we stood on the balcony of the air station and watched the plane, first of all maneuvering into position, then taking off, and becoming smaller and smaller in the clear sky. We stood there until it was only the tiniest spot and until it completely disappeared.

We have never watched a plane so intently for so long in all our lives. I never knew that it could be held by the eyes for so long. Indeed, love held it. This is how we are holding you in our hearts and shall to the end of our lives. Though you have left, our services for the Lord are richer, fuller and more blessed, and the memories are exquisite.

The Peoples Church feels very near, real and precious. We are praying for it, its beloved Pastors, leaders in the fields of the world, a richer and fuller blessing to all connected with your church, for your ministry through your books and magazines.

Yours in His love,
Hans von Staden

9

Paul in the Pulpit

Oswald continued to pastor the church for three more years after his trip to South Africa. Paul had now worked as associate pastor alongside his father for seven years.

Driving home in the car one evening after an inspiring service in The Peoples Church, Daisy, though not given to flattery, could scarcely restrain the sense of joy that welled up within her as she thought of the tributes paid to Oswald by his elders, as many of them testified in the meeting and expressed their appreciation for blessings received through his ministry. Turning to him, she said, "Wasn't that a wonderful, rewarding service? Did you ever think the work would grow to such proportions? I would say you are at the very peak of your ministry right now."

"Yes," he said happily; then changing rapidly to a solemn mood, "But Daisy, I have something I should tell you. For some time now I have been in much prayer considering my resignation as pastor of The Peoples Church."

Daisy was stunned and exclaimed, "You, resign, at sixty-nine years of age? You wouldn't resign! You would

177

just shift gears, and I don't mean a lower gear either! I mean you would work harder than ever! Oswald, why on earth would you retire as pastor now just when the work is forging ahead?"

"I want to give the work to Paul while everything is going well. I would still be around if he wanted any advice. Also I could pursue my evangelistic and missionary ministry more, embarking on a whole new program for God as an ambassador for missions around the world."

They parked the car in the garage and entered their home. An unavoidable silence prevailed as they were both preoccupied with their own mixed feelings and thoughts. Daisy, still recovering from the shock of Oswald's abrupt announcement, walked into the living room to find him pacing back and forth as he continued to ponder the importance of his decision. Unaware that Daisy was in the room, he was startled by her sudden outburst when she said forcefully, "Oswald, sit down! I want to talk to you." Though Oswald would have preferred to continue walking back and forth, he reluctantly sat down in his favorite chair, where he could at least rock back and forth, nervously adjusting his tie, impatiently awaiting what she had to say.

Although deep down in her heart she had hoped Paul would eventually succeed his father, she began, "It's hard, Oswald, for me to picture Paul as pastor. It seems only yesterday he graduated from college. It is even more difficult to realize you would not be the head of that great work God gave to us, but, on the other hand, what greater reward could come to our hearts than to know the charge would be passed on to our son?" Her remarks drew no response, as Oswald, in his customary manner, remained silent, deep in thought. Daisy became equally quiet. She had a faraway look in her eyes as conflicting thoughts raced through her mind.

"I have been the pastor's wife, and now I would become the pastor's mother. All these years I have carried the burden of the work for my husband, and now I will be carrying it for my son. I would never be able to divorce myself from the intense interest I have in it. Surely this is too much to expect of any one woman!" she thought, with a deep sigh. She continued on in her thoughts, "What if the people like Paul better than his father? I would not like that! What if they felt he was a disappointment after his father? I sure wouldn't like that either!"

"Daisy, you are very quiet. What are you thinking?"

"Nothing, Oswald, but your shoes are pretty big ones for anyone to fill, you know, especially your own son."

"But Daisy, don't forget, he's got a lot of you in him as well."

"I don't know whether that is good or bad," she replied. "Well, then," as if seeing more clearly the dawning of a new era in their lives, she went on, "of this one thing we can be sure. Paul has been destined to take over the work from his childhood days when he sang on the platform. God has blessed him with unusual gifts which I am sure will have far-reaching effects. He has been your associate for seven years now," she reasoned, "and he is thirty-seven, which is a good age for him to get settled in a pastorate." Then with deep conviction she concluded, "It will be a real transition for us, but somehow I feel it is just the beginning of a new and ever widening ministry."

The auditorium was charged with excitement and

great expectancy that memorable night in January 1959, and yet for many who had known only Oswald as their pastor the atmosphere was punctuated by feelings of nostalgia. This induction service was unique as it was honoring two personalities, father and son, who had in their own winning way captured the love and respect of the congregation.

As the building vibrated with the singing of Oswald's hymn, "The Song of the Soul Set Free," the founder and his wife, followed by their younger son Paul and Anita, his wife, took their seats on the platform. Moments later, Oswald requested the congregation to stand while he, noticeably moved with deep emotion, began reading from I Chronicles 28:9, 10, 20—David's charge to his son Solomon.

> And thou, Solomon my son, know thou the God of thy father, and serve Him with a perfect heart and with a willing mind; for the Lord searcheth all hearts, and understandeth all the imaginations of the thoughts; if thou seek Him, He will be found of thee; Take heed now; for the Lord hath chosen thee to build an house for the sanctuary: be strong, and do it. . . .
> And David said to Solomon his son, Be strong and of good courage, and do it: fear not, nor be dismayed; for the Lord God, even my God, will be with thee; He will not fail thee, nor forsake thee, until thou hast finished all the work for the service of the house of the Lord.

At the end of this solemn charge the board of managers (the executive governing power of The Peoples Church) in a traditional manner gathered around their new pastor to lay hands upon him as the prayer of dedication was offered.

During those hallowed moments, a silence crept over the audience of more than two thousand people, gripped and moved by this sacred sight. Paul, still bowed in prayer, overwhelmed by the awesome responsibility of the authority invested in him, thought of how Elijah had wrapped his mantle of power about the shoulders of Elisha. He prayed that a double portion of God's spirit would likewise rest upon his ministry.

In these solemn moments, Daisy, realizing the sacrifices required to be a true helpmate in the ministry, lifted her heart in silent prayer for her daughter-in-law Anita.

In response to the prayer of dedication the congregation sang sincerely from their hearts, "Make Him a Blessing."

Rising to speak, Paul reflected over the ministry of the past thirty years. To his parents' surprise, he asked them to step forward and stand on either side of him. Placing one arm around his father and the other around his devoted mother, he requested the congregation to rise to their feet in a moment of silent prayer, returning thanks to God for the spiritual blessings received under their ministry. As his parents stood beside him, he had arranged for the building to be in darkness except for a single light over the pulpit. Standing in the darkness with this brilliant light focused upon them, they symbolized the light lit years ago that had since penetrated to the ends of the earth. The stillness was broken by the congregation singing triumphantly, "Praise God from Whom All Blessings Flow."

Paul's mother could never forget the powerful sermon he preached that night on "How God Kept a Preacher's Son." She remembered how she had agonized so long in prayer for his faith in God to be restored. As she listened, her mind went back to the days when he was a small boy playing church, preaching to Hope and Glen, a congregation of two. Little did she know then, some day his congregation would number over two thousand!

Before she retired that night, she looked in the mirror. Removing her little flowered lavender hat, she thought of another occasion many years ago when she had pulled her deaconess' bonnet firmly on her head and asserted that she was *bound to be free*! So much had taken place since then. How thankful she was for the freedom she had chosen, since she knew for one thing she would never have had a son to carry on their ministry if she had not decided to bind herself to husband and home.

"What a reward!" she thought. "Paul is in the pulpit."

It was January 1959. Oswald was sixty-nine, Paul had turned thirty-eight, and Daisy was still the human power behind the throne.

Although Daisy enjoyed her trip abroad, she was glad to get home and catch up on all that had happened in the lives of her children and grandchildren in her absence.

She was just beginning to enjoy her reunion with them when school ended for the summer and they all took off from hot, humid Toronto for their cottages, about one hundred and twenty miles from the city. Daisy disliked this time of the year because she begrudged the nearly three months apart from them.

She learned to drive in their first car, a Star, during the "Roaring Twenties" and she decided one day to pay a visit to the lake. She hated to miss the growing-up years since lately she was traveling with Oswald more.

The pine-scented air coming in through the open window of the car as she drove through the narrow woodland road was mixed with the faint, sweet fragrance of clover and wild flowers. A brilliant light from the warm summer sun crowned the head of the golden dandelions and buttercups happily swaying in the breeze. Intermingled with the white birch trees, the maples formed a canopy overhead as she journeyed along the rushing river. Chipmunks and rabbits hopped across the road in a frolicking mood, scampering into the bushes as if in a hurry to join the rest of their woodland friends. The rushing of the river over the rocks along with the singing of the birds high in the treetops added to the music of all nature as she slowly wended her way down the winding road, eventually arriving at the water's edge.

A nostalgic feeling encompassed her as she recalled taking Chrissie and her three children to the cottage every year when school was over while Oswald spoke at conferences in the United States during the summer months. It seemed like yesterday her children were small and now here she was going to visit their children. Daisy realized as never before how swiftly life moves along.

Surrounded by all this beauty she tried to visualize what heaven must be like. The verse that came to her as she stopped the car and looked across the lake was I Corinthians 2:9—"... Eye hath not seen, nor ear heard, neither have entered into the heart of man, the things which God hath prepared for them that love Him." Though this earth was beautiful, one could never imagine what heaven would be like.

As she walked up the path to the cottage, she was greeted by hugs, kisses and the sight of the happy faces of her grandchildren who had been anxiously awaiting her arrival. "What a wonderful end to my journey!" she thought as she embraced one and then the other in turn.

Each one had so much to tell her and show her—the model boats they had made, the twenty frogs they had caught in the creek beside the cottage for bait, the big fish they had hooked, and numerous stories about the fish that got away.

The next morning was Sunday. Bright sunshine flooded her room, and she was soon awakened by the sound of happy little voices, of lively children eagerly awaiting breakfast so that they could see their beloved "Dais." After breakfast, other children accompanied by their parents arrived to visit.

While the children were playing together, Daisy sat on the dock by the water and talked with the parents, John and Betty Brooks. They had brought their water skis and were planning a Sunday of skiing after a swim in the warm waters of the lake. "Since today is the Lord's Day," said Daisy, "would there be a little church we could attend nearby?"

"There is a little church on the lake, but frankly, I have never seen any reason to go to church, Mrs. Smith. Don't you think one can worship God just as well here on the dock or golfing or fishing?"

"No, I do not," Daisy replied emphatically. "When people golf or fish they don't worship God. They are doing what they want to do—golf or fish. God says in His Word, 'Not forsaking the assembling of ourselves together...' (Hebrews 10:25). I believe we need to meet as a body of Christians to hear the Word, pray, sing, and have fellowship one with another. Everyone should do this at least once a week."

"But what do you feel is the primary function of the

organized church other than what you have mentioned?" he questioned, becoming interested in what Daisy had to say.

"Its function is to present the gospel to those who have not heard or accepted it and prepare them to spend eternity in heaven by accepting what Christ did for them on the cross."

"Why else is it important?" he asked, obviously feeling a bit uneasy since he was not accustomed to attending church.

"In unity is power, Mr. Brooks. It is necessary for Christians to unite in one common bond. The first church was formed in Jerusalem. God thought it important enough to mention in the Bible. It says in Acts 2:1, ' . . . they were all with one accord in one place.' That was when the Holy Spirit came upon them."

John picked up his skis and as he was slipping his foot into the first one, he paused and turned to Daisy again as if he could not get enough to satisfy his searching heart. He asked, "But, Mrs. Smith, how important is it to a Christian who knows the gospel to keep going to church regularly?"

"Very important. Once a Christian starts staying away from church, he begins to drift away from God and His teachings." Betty, who had been listening intently, interrupted, "I understand that your husband is a missionary statesman and that you travel abroad with him. What would you say a missionary is anyway?"

"A missionary is a vehicle conveying the gospel to a lost world wherever he goes. God sometimes shows the need of a whole country as He did to the apostle Paul. He heard God's voice saying, 'Come over into Macedonia, and help us'" (Acts 16:9). Daisy found it incredible that some people did not know the definition of a missionary.

John, taking off his skis, continued, "Tell me, what makes a good missionary?"

"One who has given his all and is willing to go wherever he is called. When a person gives up the comforts of this life and obeys a call to the jungle or some other remote part of the world because of his dedication and devotion to Christ, and because of a compassion for the lost, or when he surrenders all to serve anywhere God leads him, at home or abroad, he is a true missionary. Without this kind of dedication a missionary is of no value."

Daisy thought all the questions were over when Betty spoke up again, "Mrs. Smith, I wish you would tell me something. When you first meet someone, what do you look for as the distinguishing traits of a Christian?"

"I must be honest with you," said Daisy. "One cannot always tell a Christian for certain. Many have lived in homes where they have heard, and are familiar with a Christian vocabulary; consequently, we assume they are Christians. A new creature in Christ is a Christian. The Bible says, in II Corinthians 5:17, 'Old things are passed away; behold, all things are become new.' Jesus said, in Matthew 7:21, 'Not every one that saith unto me, Lord, Lord, shall enter into the kingdom of heaven; but he that doeth the will of my Father which is in heaven.' God's Word also states that 'the Spirit itself beareth witness with our spirit, that we are the children of God'" (Romans 8:16).

"Christians speak as Christians because the Bible says in Luke 6:45, 'Of the abundance of the heart his mouth speaketh.' A Christian does not swear or take God's name in vain when he is under stress, because it is not in his heart to do so. On the other hand, it is doubtful whether someone who does take God's name in vain is a Christian. Bitter and sweet water do not come from the same fountain.

"Christians do not slander other people. I used to tell my children they should ask themselves three questions before criticizing anyone. First, is it kind? Second, is it true? Third, is it necessary?"

"You have given us a lot to think about today, Mrs. Smith," said Betty. "John, why don't we start going to church regularly and learn more about all of this?"

I am willing, Betty. I don't like to think of our children growing up without knowing anything about being Christians," he said thoughtfully.

"Do you mind if we come to talk to you again?" he asked as he picked up his skis and climbed into the boat, forgetting his original intention to go skiing.

"It is not what I say or think that matters, Mr. Brooks. It is what the Bible says, and the best thing you can do is to read it and live by its teachings. I can assure you of one thing. I will pray that God will illuminate His Word to you, and that you will experience the need and joy of attending church."

"We will read the Bible," he said, as the children jumped into the boat. Daisy watched them speed away across the lake after an inspiring visit which had been totally unexpected when they first arrived that Sunday morning.

Daisy knew then that God had not brought her to the lake just to visit her grandchildren, but He wanted to use her in some small way to influence the lives of these young parents by answering their searching questions.

The happy week of inspiration, sunshine, blue skies, joy and laughter came to an end, and Daisy was sad to leave her loved ones, and return to the hustle and bustle of the hot city with all of its many demands and cares.

10

South America

With Paul now in full charge as pastor, Oswald was looking to God for the next thing on the program for him when he opened the mail one morning and read a letter inviting him to hold meetings in all the major cities of South America. The aim of the crusade was to stir up churches to do more for missions, and lead the Christians into a deeper experience with God.

When he arrived home from the office, he placed the letter in Daisy's hands, and said enthusiastically, "How would you like to go to South America with me? I am sure you could be a blessing to many women on that great continent."

"South America! That would be wonderful. What a long way God has brought me from my first mission field in West Virginia!" she thought as she read the letter. She had been faithful in her work, and now God, through her husband, was extending her ministry to large groups of women in foreign lands. After prayer and preparation, Daisy and Oswald took off once more to serve their Lord and Master.

Their first stop was Rio de Janeiro, Brazil's second largest city and its cultural center. As they flew over, it seemed to be surrounded by sea and mountains, some rising up from the center of the city. It was a maze of valleys, inlets, and white beaches with rugged rocks plunging dramatically to the shore.

Above all the mountains, twenty-three hundred feet high stood the Hunchback, from which a ninety-foot statue of Christ the Redeemer looked down. The city was founded five hundred years before and had over four million people. As Daisy gazed up at this statue, she wished everyone knew the One it represented as she knew Him.

Driving through Rio, Daisy noticed women kissing each other on both cheeks when they met, and men embracing in friendship. People in Canada seemed so cold and hard in contrast to the warm, friendly people of Rio de Janeiro. Daisy thought of the verse of Scripture, "Behold how they love one another." One would think they were Christians because of the love they demonstrated for each other. She thought what wonderful Christians these people would make if they once received the love of God into their hearts.

After capacity crowds and 109 decisions for Christ in the different churches, they moved on to Sao Paulo—where they were welcomed by the Canadian consul and his wife in an auditorium seating seven thousand people. The building was crowded every night and the mayor presented them with the gold key to the city at the end of their meetings in appreciation of their ministry.

The next stop was Curitba. As they stepped off the plane, Daisy was overwhelmed to see a great choir singing songs of welcome at the airport. They were taken almost immediately to their hotel and then to the evening service. In an auditorium seating four thousand, five and six thousand managed to press their way into the building; many had to stand up throughout the three-hour service.

While the soloist was singing one of Oswald's hymns, "The Glory of His Presence," he was interrupted by a great crash, as one whole section of the overcrowded gallery gave way, injuring many of the people. Nurses and doctors and many ambulances were sent for to attend to the wounded. Daisy was afraid the meeting would have to end, but the rest of the crowd insisted that it proceed. As soon as those who were hurt were taken from the building, order was restored and the service continued.

At the close of the meeting, which proved to be a fruitful one, hundreds responded to the invitation to accept Christ, and the police had to clear a path for Daisy and Oswald to get through to their waiting car. God overruled the dramatic events of the evening and the publicity in the papers resulted in drawing larger crowds the next night. Daisy felt that this accident was a reminder of the uncertainty of life on earth and made the crowd eager to respond to the message and prepare for eternity.

The mayor, accompanied by an army general, who happened to be a Christian, took Daisy and Oswald to visit the governor in his private mansion. They had a wonderful opportunity to talk with him of their work in Canada. Afterwards he gave them an autographed book to remind them of the work accomplished in their city for God.

Leaving Curitba, they held meetings in Montevideo, Rosario, Santiago and then to Buenos Aires, capital of Argentina. Buenos Aires in many ways resembled Paris.

Counting the suburbs it had a population of seven million. There were costly mansions as well as huge slums and unfinished housing developments. Buenos Aires was the great dynamic heartbeat of Argentina.

Argentina had a large population of Indians, some who were born there, and others who had crossed the border from Chile and descended the steep trails of the Andes. Four or five million people known as mestizos, or people of mixed ancestry, lived on the pampas away from the large cities. Many of them traveled long distances to attend the services in the city. The meetings were held in a stadium seating twenty-five thousand people. Ten thousand stood all through the service every night. There was some opposition in that city. Other religious groups flew over the city and dropped leaflets warning people not to attend the meetings. This aroused curiosity and succeeded in increasing the attendance.

Every night at the close of the services the women would come up and kiss Oswald's hand to show their gratitude for his messages. Mothers held their children to be kissed as well. Each night they presented Daisy with a huge bouquet of flowers, making her feel appreciated and warmly welcomed. Daisy graciously received the flowers and was deeply impressed by the kindness and affection of the people.

Many remarkable conversions took place. Daisy was told of a man who had started out from home with a gun in his pocket, intending to commit suicide. He heard singing as he was walking past the stadium and decided to go in. When the singing was over he listened intently to the message of eternal life in Christ. He had never heard anything like it before. He thought that if he shot himself life would come to an end and he did not know this would mean living on in torment and separation from God. At the close he responded to the invitation, gave his gun to the personal worker that was leading him to Christ, and was filled with a peace and joy he had never known before. He no longer had the desire to commit suicide. Daisy said, if they had come all the way from Canada in order that this one man should find the Savior, it was worth the trip.

Every night the crowds grew larger. Some from distances of five hundred miles had heard about the meetings and had come to the city to attend; others came from the flat and dusty, sun-baked pampas far to the west. Each night an air of expectancy ran through the crowd like invisible fire. The hum of voices before the service started was like a hive of bees on a summer's day. The swelling wave of music from thousands of inspired souls was like the sound of many waters. Daisy was astonished to see people going up and down the aisles, before the service began, selling candy, and drinks, as they would at a ball game. This was something she had never seen in a Christian service.

It was no ordinary crowd of fight fans that habitually filled the stadium. There was no blue haze of tobacco smoke, no shouting, and no applause; for this was another kind of battle, a spiritual struggle between the forces of Christ and the hosts of Satan. No blood was spattered on the canvas floor of the ring, but history was made as the campaign progressed. The powerful ministry was like sledge-hammer blows smashing against Satan's walls erected in the hearts of men.

At one of the services Oswald offered to autograph his hymn books for the choir. A terrible crash was heard and Daisy found herself, along with everyone else that had been sitting on the platform, suddenly transferred to the floor with a thud. The whole platform had fallen in under the weight of the people and Daisy looked around in horror, not quite knowing what had happened. To her amazement she caught sight of Oswald continuing to autograph the books, unmoved by, and paying no attention to, the catastrophe.

As they made their way inch by inch to the car, through the pressing crowds, young and old embraced them, children kissed them, and when the police on duty to protect them helped them into the car, crowds reached their hands through the windows and threw flowers into the car. Never in all her life had Daisy seen such enthusiasm, love, and friendship. The South American people had beautiful ways of expressing themselves and Daisy felt their love wherever she went. She addressed large meetings for women with buildings crowded to capacity. Their hunger for the gospel inspired her as she stood before them preaching a message that had been heard so often in Canada but was like new wine to those people. Whenever she spoke at a meeting someone would pin an exquisite orchid on her, one of the many gestures of their love and appreciation.

Mrs. Rosenberg Spitzer, a talented linguist, was largely responsible for organizing their meetings in South America and Daisy and Oswald deeply appreciated her efforts. Volunteers covered the city with red and black handbills and posters announcing the meetings. Forty Christian men put their cars at the disposal of the advertising committee which organized a parade of cars draped with the eye-catching red and black posters, routing them through the main sections of the city.

The great stadium in Buenos Aires had been the scene of wrestling matches. It had now become the mecca towards which multitudes of people headed from the subways. As the throngs stepped off the subways, which were covered with such gospel texts as, "Look unto Me and be ye saved," they were singing Oswald's song, "Joy in Serving Jesus."

The gallery seats were nothing better than hard cement steps. It was not the beauty of the sanctuary that attracted the crowds, but the hunger for the simplicity and directness of Oswald's sermons. His messages appealed to their understanding and moved hearts to respond.

"You know, Mrs. Smith," said one of the ministers, "when your husband speaks he seems to be speaking directly and individually to each person. I notice a power operating in his life that could not be mistaken for psychology or the natural gift of a great preacher. This is what appeals to our people." Daisy's heart was thrilled to know that the Holy Spirit was so evident in her husband's ministry.

After weeks of strenuous meetings, speaking so constantly, Oswald had contracted a bad chest cold, and they were forced to have a week's rest. A multimillionaire, who employed one thousand men in his factory, entertained them in his villa located in the foothills of the Andes in Chile. Their souls and bodies daily absorbed the beauty and warmth of the indescribable sunsets, the flowers, and beautiful shady trees at the foot of the snowclad mountains. Their host, the Swiss consul, and his wife could not have done more for them during their rest week between campaigns. Once again one of Daisy's favorite verses proved true—"Seek ye first the kingdom of God and His righteousness; and all these things shall be added unto you" (Matthew 6:33).

After great victories in Buenos Aires they flew to Lima, the capital of the Republic of Peru, more Spanish than any other South American capital. A most distinctive city, Lima had retained its aura of the past while keeping up with the new.

The finer residential districts of Lima are among the most beautiful in the world. As they drove through this modern city, they observed that some of the ornate summer homes of the last century survived the Chilean occupation of 1881-83 and were still in use.

Other dwellings called *callejones* were situated in long alleys. They were street-level apartments dating from colonial days and were made of mud over a base of woven cane, then painted in pastel colors, durable in a rainless climate.

Over 100,000 Indians from the sierra had marched into unoccupied land in Lima and erected shacks. These were built of bamboo mats, mud bricks, or collapsed oil drums, but later the government offered them prefabricated housing for seven dollars per month.

People from all of these different areas, including hundreds from the modern part of Lima, thronged to the meetings.

In Lima they opened with a great service in the Coliseum, seating six thousand people, but on the fourth night the archbishop of a large denomination invoked a decree that forbade religious meetings in public places and got a government official to ban them. Peru was the only country in all South America where such interference was encountered, but Daisy had a chance to speak to a large group of women in Lima. How she loved to minister to these women who were so responsive to her convicting message!

God used both of them to give the churches of South America a new missionary vision and their hearts were filled with gratitude to Him as they boarded the plane for Miami and home once again.

11

On the Move

The Peoples Church, purchased thirty years before, was now over one hundred years old. A minimum of repair work had been done to prevent it from falling down or being condemned by the city. The floor of the main auditorium was still rough lumber and the only finishing material that had ever been put on it was the carpet that ran down the main aisles. The building was badly in need of paint and the brick work on the outside was in poor condition.

The reason so little was spent on the building was that in the past thirty years seven dollars was sent overseas for every one dollar spent on the budget of the home base. Now God was going to reward the congregation for their faithfulness to the cause of foreign missions by making it possible for them to move to a new location and put up a modern building with all of the facilities necessary for the work.

Paul had been pastor for over two years and the Sunday night crowds always overtaxed the capacity of the church. He now had to get adequate educational facilities to take care of the growing needs of a modern Sunday school.

After a period of thirty years of concentration on foreign missions, God turned the original $75,000 investment in the old church into a sum more than eight times as large—$650,000.

Paul hurried over to see his parents on their arrival home. His father was out, but he always enjoyed discussing his plans with his mother as well, and could hardly wait to tell her about the new building he was planning to erect.

"Do you realize, Mother," Paul said, as he arrived just in time for a cup of afternoon tea (a regular custom in the Smith household), "that the congregation will have to raise only about $75,000 for the furnishings and the equipment?"

"This is too good to be true, Paul. Will the people still have to park blocks from the church as they do now?" she asked.

"Wait until you see the size of the parking lot!" he exclaimed. "It will accommodate three hundred cars on the church property."

"How many will the new building seat?" asked Daisy, her mind spinning with so many questions.

"It will be built in the shape of a huge fan with a balcony that goes around three sides. I expect to seat twenty-five hundred people and, with extra chairs, three thousand. Mother, the choir loft alone will seat one hundred and twenty people!" he said excitedly as he visualized his dream coming into being.

"What about the Sunday school? Will you have room

for it to grow? It is the future church and it would be wonderful if you could expand it."

"For the first time in the history of the church, we will have adequate educational facilities so that the Sunday school can be completely departmentalized and we will be able to more than double its enrolment.

Then Daisy came to the most important question in her mind. "You won't let the missionary work suffer, will you, with all that must be done for the church? Always remember this was the reason for founding the work and the reason it has prospered."

"You never need to remind me of that, Mother. I share the same vision as you and Dad, and I can assure you it will not suffer. Because of the increase in numbers in our congregation we will be able to expand our missionary program. Instead of sharing in the support of three hundred and fifty missionaries, I am expecting to increase it to four hundred on the mission field. I am standing on the promise found in Haggai 2:9 where God said, 'The glory of this latter house shall be greater than of the former. . . .'"

Daisy's heart was filled with gratitude to God to think that her son was going to continue to carry out the vision they had always had for the church to put foreign missions first.

"I think we need another cup of tea to digest all of that," she said, as she reached for the teapot.

"That is not all," said Paul. "Mother, since Dad will be away on the Sunday afternoon we intend to turn the first sod for the new church, I want you to come and represent him at that service and turn the sod for us."

Filled with emotion, and a feeling of honor and gratitude, Daisy assured him she would be present, and overjoyed to turn the first sod.

At three o'clock on the designated Sunday afternoon nearly three thousand people gathered for the ceremony. The thing that impressed Daisy the most was to see all the people marching around the four-and-a-half acres as they claimed the promise in Deuteronomy 11:24 which says, "Every place whereon the soles of your feet shall tread shall be your's. . . ."

They walked around in silence as they prayed. Daisy realized she was not just witnessing a twentieth-century miracle, but was participating in it. Only the thousands of people actually on the scene could fully appreciate the electric atmosphere of that historic day. All Daisy could say was, "To God Be the Glory."

The first building fund convention was launched and the offering was received in an atmosphere charged with excitement; Paul announced a total of $75,000. The people who gave this amount were already giving over $360,000 for foreign missions. God was proving His faithfulness and it was marvelous in the eyes of all on Sunday, October 28, 1962, when they moved into the church that to them was a miracle, a church of that size free of debt.

The last Sunday at the old church left a lasting impression on everyone. Paul preached in the morning and Oswald preached at night on "Ten Stops to Bloor Street." The first two stops were in his twenties, Dale Church and Beulah Tabernacle. The next six were in his thirties. The last two were in his forties.

Daisy, faithfully standing by her husband's side, was asked to speak at the close of his message. She told how she had met Oswald at the first stop—Dale Church. She was so overcome with joy and gratefulness to God for all He had done since that first stop that she could not keep the tears back as she traced His hand at each stop throughout her life. The lights went out for the last time in the old church, and the next Sunday began a new era.

12

The Orient

It was the centenary of missions in Tokyo, Japan. Oswald was overjoyed to receive an invitation to represent Canada in this historic event. Daisy had always dreamed of visiting a country where the customs, culture and language were entirely different from Canada. Now her dream was to be realized as she had been invited to go along with her husband to this fascinating country.

They were met in Tokyo by a Japanese Christian couple, Mr. and Mrs. Ohi, who greeted their Canadian visitors by bowing graciously and smiling broadly. Mr. Ohi demonstrated great respect for Oswald because of his snow white hair. Japanese people feel men with white hair must be full of wisdom and authority. Mrs. Ohi resembled a Japanese doll in her colorful kimono, a style of dress not worn by all women in Japan for many have adopted Western fashions. She was petite and especially beautiful when she smiled. Daisy was fascinated with her appearance and manner.

While discussing Japanese customs and culture as

they drove towards Tokyo, Daisy turned to Mr. Ohi and asked, "Did your parents choose your wife for you?"

"Oh, yes," replied Mr. Ohi, "but I did not have to marry her. My parents paid fifty dollars to an investigator to look into the background of several other girls, but I refused to marry them even though they came up to my parents' requirements for my wife. I finally decided to marry Sumi because she was from a good family and she was healthy. After we were married about a year, I fell in love with her, as you would say. She is a good wife, aren't you, Sumi?" he said proudly as her reached over and squeezed her hand.

Daisy braced herself as they approached Tokyo and proceeded through the unbelievably busy, cramped and winding streets. She was continually jolted as Mr. Ohi slammed on his brakes trying to dodge the multitudes of pedestrians. Other drivers had little regard for traffic laws—they ran red lights regularly, ignored stop signs and exceeded speed limits. The city appeared to have no plan, but just fanned out in circles from the Imperial Palace with radial roads stretching out as the city had grown.

Nearly one-fifth of Japan's people were living in Tokyo and its suburbs. Twice it had been nearly destroyed—in 1923 by a great earthquake, and in 1945 by Allied bombings. Each time it was rebuilt with no order to its layout.

"How often do you have earthquakes here?" asked Daisy, feeling a little insecure.

"This city is threatened by ten mild tremors daily with a more severe one every few weeks. Buildings are uninteresting here compared to your country," replied Mr. Ohi. "These gray concrete structures can not be built more than ten stories high because of the danger of earth-quakes." It was a gloomy-looking city to Daisy as a thick smog engulfed it, making it look more gray than ever.

For all its modern or Western appearance, Tokyo still had the Shinto shrines, the little dark geisha tea rooms, and the boutiques selling hand-sewn kimonos. A legacy of tradition and culture was evident on every side, making the mood and style of the city different and unique. On the other hand, the city was filled with modern department stores, hotels and subways, just as in Canada and the United States.

Down the narrow, twisting, wandering lanes they drove, past the homes and shops, the fronts of which came to the edge of the road where children tried to play and neighbors visited their friends. Daisy thought, as she looked at them, of the struggle they must have just to find space to live, to work, to move, to eat, to sleep or even to think. They seemed bound and hampered on every side, knowing nothing of freedom to enjoy spacious gardens and parks, or large properties surrounding their dwellings.

Mr. Ohi, as many other Japanese people whom Daisy met, was tense. She felt this was due to the continous movement in the city; the friction over space put great pressure on the personalities of Tokyo people. Even their subways made Canadian subways seem as empty and spacious as the prairies.

The drive suddenly came to an end as they stopped in front of a hotel where they were to have their first Japanese dinner.

Seated on a cushion on the floor, Daisy found chop sticks very hard to use as she tried to transport the raw fish and various other Japanese dishes from her plate to her mouth. "My problem," said Daisy, "is that with these chop sticks the food is cold by the time it reaches its destination." Mrs. Ohi had been in the United States on a visit and realized how difficult it must be for Daisy to manipulate this form of cutlery. She tried to teach her how to pick up the food but without much success.

After dinner, Mr. Ohi left his guests at their hotel, which was located near the Imperial Palace, where the Emperor and his family reside. The words for Emperor (*tennor heika*) mean literally, "under the steps to the throne of the heavenly sovereign." He is the supplicant for the Japanese people to their gods. They consider his person sacred and reverence him, but no longer feel he is divine. They believe in the teachings of Buddhism and they think that Shinto spirits have influence over their crops and steel mills. They worship their ancestors still, and though the gospel first came to their country one hundred years ago, they are bound by superstitions, and the worship of idols. "What a tragedy," thought Daisy, as she listened to Mr. Ohi tell something of their beliefs. He was so thrilled to give testimony of the renunciation in his life of all this and the new joy and freedom he had in knowing Christ. He was grateful that missionaries had brought the gospel one hundred years ago, although Jesus was still unknown to so many.

The next day was Sunday, and as Mr. and Mrs. Ohi picked Daisy and Oswald up for church, Daisy noticed that all the stores were open and realized more than ever that she was not in a Christian country.

The churches were very small and the people were squeezed together on benches. Straw mats covered the floor and some were kneeling on them. After several had led in prayer, all the people were invited to pray audibly together, each in his own words. They started off in a low rumble which became louder and louder until their voices reached quite a roar. After the leader stopped praying, complete silence prevailed. It reminded Daisy of a clap of thunder followed by a rumbling off in the distance.

It was a very old church—it had been built in 1872. What a thrill for Daisy to notice Oswald's books printed in Japanese on the tables in the front! They were served cups (without handles) of green tea before each service. They had inspiring services with the Japanese people and many were brought to Jesus Christ.

Mr. Ohi called for them at their hotel and took them to the train to visit the city of Nagoya. The train was air-conditioned with a radio set and earphones at each seat. Japanese hostesses made the trip comfortable and enjoyable. Oswald appreciated the fact that the trains were punctual and dependable. Daisy gave out tracts to those seated around her in the coach and they seemed grateful to receive them. She noticed expressions of sadness and hopelessness on many faces and that made her long to give them the message of freedom in Christ which she knew. She would not know if any came to know Christ through the reading of the tracts, but at least she was faithful in scattering the seed.

Daisy would never be able to erase the sight she encountered as she stepped off the train in Nagoya. A terrible typhoon had struck just a few days before and now they saw an indescribable sight of destruction and misery. Hundreds of homes were flat on the ground. Blankets and quilts were spread out to dry on the top of the houses still standing. The water had risen to about the first story and the people were compelled to climb on top of the roofs to save their lives.

It was a scene of almost total destruction as if a bomb had been dropped. It was estimated that 451,000 homes were destroyed. Bridges were washed away, ships sunk, airplanes demolished. Great breakers crashed against the sea wall and splashed up over the highways.

"Look at those long lines of people waiting for relief, Oswald," cried Daisy as she watched the hopeless people waiting for food and clothing piled up in the relief centers. "What are those soldiers looking for through all that rubbish and ruin?" she asked, as the missionary who had accompanied them led them closer to the destruction.

"They are searching for bodies of their missing relatives." Coffins were piled one on top of the other. Daisy watched as Red Cross workers were opening the coffins. They lifted up a corpse by the shoulders and the feet and then laid it on a mat while relatives and friends gathered to see if they could identify it.

Pieces of clothing were fastened to a wall in the hope that someone would recognize them. Dysentery was breaking out everywhere and all the water had to be boiled. The full fury and destruction could never be described. Thousands were starving, wet and naked. Some of them were clinging to the rafters of their homes, frantic with fear and cold. All the lights had gone out; for two days no help had come.

Daisy thought of a Chinese proverb she had once heard: "That which is seen with the eye is never forgotten in the heart." The tragedy of that scene would ever remain vivid in her heart. "To think," she exclaimed, "we were safe in a hotel in Tokyo unaware of this awful devastation and loss—families separated and wiped out, water flowing fifteen miles from the coast, flooding the entire territory and here a week later it is still above the floor of the church!"

In her hotel room that night, Daisy thought of the dramatic heart-rending scenes of the day. She was reminded that Christians have a wonderful hope for the future. While this loss and destruction she had seen was unbelievably sad, it was nothing compared to the millions on earth who are going into a Christless eternity every day. People in Canada were holding the truth smugly to themselves, just as she had sat safe and sound in the hotel unaware of terrible loss being experienced all around. The sight of Nagoya had given Daisy a new burden for those dying without ever hearing the name of Jesus, who had died to save them for all eternity. She felt depressed and unusually burdened as she knelt in prayer for those without Christ. Suddenly there was a knock at the door.

Opening the door, she was greeted by a tiny Japanese man who, bowing graciously, informed her that she was wanted on the phone. She followed him to the phone at the end of the hall, and picking it up, her heavy heart was suddenly filled with joy as she heard Glen speaking to her from a city just five hundred miles away. Glen and his wife, Kay, were on their way to India where he was going to lecture in the hospitals to doctors, nurses, and medical students.

Daisy's spirit was uplifted to hear her elder son's voice when she was so far from home and loved ones. God had His own wonderful way of bringing joy to her heart on the heels of sorrow.

Osaka was the next Japanese city where they were to visit and hold meetings. Not far from Osaka is Nara, a serene little town filled with temples, pagodas and parks with tame deer roaming in the countryside. It was such a relief to see a quiet town in Japan with places to walk and think. Nara was surrounded by gleaming white temples with pebbled courtyards. In the city itself, nestled against the hillside, stood an exquisite shrine with vermilion gates, green grass and white walls, a mixture of Chinese Buddhist and Japanese Shinto architecture. Each year twelve monks gathered in an upper room for a private supper and ritual. Religious scholars wonder if this originated from strains of Christianity and the Last Supper that might have reached Japan before the first European missionaries arrived. Daisy and Oswald found this a very interesting place, so different from other cities they had seen. It was like an oasis after Tokyo.

After well-attended and successful meetings in Osaka, they left for the much anticipated city of Hong Kong.

Daisy found Hong Kong a beautiful, fascinating, and paradoxical city, a magnificent port fringed with bays, peninsulas and hills rising abruptly from the sea. Several of the harbor's docks could handle vessels up to 750 feet in length, but much of the port's cargo was transported in picturesque junks of all sizes.

One thing that impressed Daisy was the many inhabitants that lived on the junks and sampans. They were called the "Boat People"; they lived (some of them for generations) and died on their boats. The sampans were like floating markets, no sails or engines, steered by one oar while the rower swings from one foot to the other. A canvas covering protects them from the strong sun.

The missionaries told Daisy and Oswald that over one hundred thousand people live on these boats, and many never set foot on land for a whole lifetime. What a work missionaries had here—giving out gospel literature to people who would never have the opportunity of entering a church or hearing the gospel! Daisy marveled at the dedication of the missionaries preaching the message of salvation under these circumstances. They were not addressing a congregation in comfortable pews from a pulpit, but spreading the good news the best way they could to souls who would otherwise be a forgotten people, the families sometimes consisting of six or seven children.

The missionaries also took Daisy to see the shacks of thousands of refugees. These people had fled to Hong Kong when the Communist government came to power in the Chinese Revolution of 1949. Unable to find lodging in this already crowded place, the refugees poured over the urban districts, squatting on the hillsides, using pieces of wood, sacking, old paraffin tins, any covering for protection. Soon the hillsides were a mass of shacks, sheltering a teeming multitude without sanitation, water mains, or light. Thousands slept on the streets. Recently the government had provided housing, or some housing improvement for about two million of them. Though it gets cold in winter in Hong Kong many of these refugees were scantily clothed. In the four- to five-foot-wide streets where they lived, chickens and ducks walked about freely. Some people were still living in hovels, but they preferred such conditions to living under Communism in Red China. For years after Daisy's visit to this area she shuddered as she thought of these people for whom Christ died and longed to see more missionaries go to bring them the good news of Jesus.

As they left this district, the missionaries took them to the little shack of a church where they were to speak. It touched Daisy's heart deeply to hear children singing Oswald's song, "Then Jesus Came," in their own language. The expressions on the faces of the converts revealed the fact that Jesus had come their way in the midst of such indescribable conditions.

In contrast to the refugee areas they also held meetings in some of the very beautiful and large auditoriums in Hong Kong. After one service they drove through magnificent scenery toward Red China until they came to a sign forbidding them to go any further. Many who had passed that sign had been arrested by the Red Guards and taken into Communist China. To Daisy it was a sobering experience to stand looking at the white houses beyond the bamboo curtain, the border where ten thousand people escaped every month. She thought of the Christians and churches in China, now under Communist rule, and of the many martyrs who had paid the supreme price. On the other side people were living bound in slavery worse than death. "If only they could know the freedom that Jesus brings when He comes," she thought. Though some had chosen to be martyrs, they had gained freedom for eternity.

The buildings chosen for the meetings could not hold the crowds. It was promised that if they would consider coming back, they could have the stadium seating thirty thousand people.

Daisy and Oswald left these wonderful people and dedicated missionaries in a country hungry for the gospel and boarded the plane for Honolulu, the paradise of the Pacific. Oswald spoke in the Kawaiahao Church which had been founded in 1820 on the spot where the missionaries commenced their work and where the kings and queens of Hawaii worshiped God. He had to remove his shoes at the door and wear a white gown in the pulpit. The choir sang from a gallery at the back, a custom in Hawaii. Fifty young people, touched by his appeal, came forward to dedicate their lives in service for God, a very unusual sight in Hawaii.

On leaving, Daisy was presented with a typical mumuu. These mumuus were introduced by missionaries who years ago found the natives without clothes. They have been a customary dress ever since.

13

A New Ministry

The tour to the Orient over, once more Daisy and Oswald returned to the work in Toronto, but for many days and nights Daisy was haunted with the thoughts of the terrible suffering and devastation she had seen in Nagoya where they had witnessed the results of the typhoon. She could not help but think of the fact that within a few days time, almost every country had responded with food, medical supplies and money, but the church had not yet supplied enough workers and distributors for the spiritual suffering all over the world.

She had a feeling of urgency to tell the women in her part of the world about conditions overseas. The church was failing to get the gospel out fast enough and she wondered what excuse would be theirs on that awful judgment day.

Daisy began to ask God for openings to speak in Canada and the United States. She wanted what she had learned in her trips abroad to bear fruit in the last days before Christ's return, which she felt were near. She was continually accepting invitations to speak at various luncheons and banquets in Canada, but longed to have her ministry broadened since time was short, and she feared soon missionaries might not be allowed to enter foreign countries.

She had been praying for some weeks, when one morning she received a letter from Dr. Jack McAlister, president of World Literature Crusade, who had visited them in South America and also in Japan. He asked if she would go to California and speak over radio and television every week during the month of May. He called it his Missionary Month for Mothers and wanted her to tell what his organization was doing at home and abroad to get the gospel to the ends of the earth. World Literature Crusade is an organization that believes strongly in the power of the printed page. Daisy's messages were to inspire people to give for the printing and distribution of tracts in foreign countries. World Literature Crusade has a staff of over two thousand native workers in two hundred and ten countries distributing Christian literature from door to door, often enduring much persecution as they walk hundreds of miles each year for Jesus' sake. This was just the opportunity Daisy had been waiting for, and she knew she must go and share all she had seen.

Television was a new experience for Daisy. Whenever she spoke, she had always been inspired by the expressions and response on the faces of her listeners, but now her audience was unseen. However, so burdened for the lost was she, that she was willing to use any method to speak with deep concern and understanding for women in foreign countries. In her first message she said:

> We wish to provide enough funds so that women missionaries working in countries where World Literature Crusade is now in action

will have at least ten dollars worth of free literature to distribute. I am desperately burdened to reach the poor lost heathen mothers.

These women live in constant dread and fear, hungry, tired and restless. They have no peace, no light and joy. Dark shadows of many gods hang constantly over them. Some have never heard of the God who breathed the breath of life into their bodies. They give alms and sacrifice to their gods, but still have no peace. They fast and pray to gods of wood and stone, and yet within their breast is no hope.

For some it may be too late. "We are too old," they say, "to forsake our many gods and search for new gods." I urge you to do what you can to help these women missionaries to reach heathen women before it is too late. They are out there waiting, waiting beyond the hills, beyond the seas, down the lonely palm forests of the jungles of Africa and South America, out in the little river boats of Hong Kong. Millions of them living in wretched poverty and squalor in thousands of villages still wait to hear the message of Christ's salvation. The Lord Jesus Christ is concerned, not only for Jerusalem and Judea, not only for Toronto, New York City or Los Angeles, His heart of compassion goes out to the uttermost parts of the earth.

These mothers have so little of this world's goods. I ask for them that you will give a little portion of the great measure which God has given to you. Your gift and your prayers will not only encourage us, but this act of faith and love on your part will help to gather in the harvest and bring God's blessing in your own soul.

After ministering for a month on television for World Literature Crusade, she came to her last message:

I'm here in behalf of the women in foreign lands, in heathen darkness where the cause of heathenism rests heaviest. These women are unwelcomed at birth, unwanted; and indeed the little life which is not destroyed in infancy grows up uncared for, unloved, considered a burden and disgrace. For her no happy childhood exists, but toil and drudgery with blows and curses. She is sold to the man who can pay the most. If she is strong she is worth a lot but if delicate she is worth little. Her misery is increased tenfold after marriage. She becomes a slave of her husband. Her life consists of bearing children and doing all the work. Even death offers no relief. She looks forward to it with superstitious dread and her sad life goes out into a sadder and more hopeless eternity.

What made our lot different? Nothing but the gospel. To know the awful need and to have available a gospel to carry to those who are needy and not do it, will result in hardening of our hearts and lives. Let me urge you who live in this land of abundance to give them the gospel before it is forever too late. Is it nothing to you that each passing day one hundred thousand go into a Christless grave, that millions die, while God in His love still calls? Seeing you have so freely received, freely give. Pledge your support to get the gospel to some of these dying women before it is too late.

Daisy's messages were challenging and right from her heart. It thrilled her to have the opportunity to speak on behalf of foreign women, to help them through the television and radio ministry open to her through World Literature Crusade. Her ministry was steadily expanding, first because of her united effort with Oswald to get the gospel out, and second because of the privilege she had of visiting many more countries, including Australia, New Zealand, Jamaica, Norway, Sweden, Denmark and Finland.

God had been mindful of her sincere efforts as a young missionary in the mountains of West Virginia; because she was faithful in a small capacity, He opened up greater and greater opportunities all the rest of her life. Daisy believed the words of Luke 12:48—". . . For unto whomsoever much is given, of him shall be much required. . . ." God had endowed her with certain talents and she was convinced that He expected her to use the ability He had given her to further His kingdom.

When she returned home from California, she received a letter from Dr. McAlister telling her how pleased he was with the results of her ministry to mothers. Because of her daily challenges many had responded and sent in money to support the work. Daisy was always careful to give God the glory for anything that had been accomplished by Him through her efforts. In response she wrote:

Dear Jack,

It was kind of you to write to me about the results of the month of May. How glad I am that it went over the top, and that it was worthwhile. It makes me happy to have had a little share in it, and as we follow it up in prayer, I am sure it will be far-reaching. Paul plants, Apollos waters, but God alone gives the increase.

Yours for missions,
Daisy

Daisy returned home from warm, sunny California, and from other parts of the United States, where she spoke to women's groups in conjunction with her husband's campaigns, to find Toronto buried in snow. After a reunion with her family at Christmas, she attended the annual watchnight service at the church on New Year's Eve. The usual baptism was held as each one gave his testimony before going into the waters of baptism.

After the baptismal service, Oswald showed his pictures of their trip to Ireland taken the previous year. Chrissie had accompanied them to Ireland, the place of her birth, and was thrilled to see the pictures of her homeland again. The service ended with the congregation partaking of communion, a beautiful and impressive service as the old year 1962 passed into history.

As they left the church to drive home, the moon was casting shadows across the field of snow in front of the church. Snowflakes drifted to earth, spreading a soft white blanket over the housetops. Daisy, Oswald, and Chrissie drove slowly home as visibility was bad and the road slippery, typical of Toronto in January.

After they reached the house, Chrissie made them a cup of tea and toast as she always did after the services.

After seeing the pictures of Ireland, Chrissie recalled her memorable trip and they shared together the blessing of the service before retiring.

Daisy had been in bed just about half an hour, when she was awakened by a loud thud on the floor. Jumping out of bed to see what it was, she made her way down the dark hall and switched on the light in the bathroom. She was utterly shocked to see their dear Chrissie lying unconscious on the floor. Immediately she wakened Oswald, and they called the doctor. When he arrived he examined Chrissie and said she had suffered a massive stroke; he called an ambulance to take her to the hospital.

After such a wonderful evening for Chrissie especially, seeing her beloved Ireland again, and enjoying such happy fellowship, it seemed incredible that she was now unconscious. Two weeks later the Lord called her to higher service. For forty-one years she had devoted herself to caring for the Smith family, faithfully ministering to their needs that they might be free to serve God. She had done nearly all the cooking for the many ministers and missionaries entertained frequently in the home. She loved their children and also their grandchildren as if they were her own. What a beautiful way to end her last conscious night on earth—seeing again scenes of the homeland from which she had journeyed many years before to find Christ and a Christian home in which to serve Him for the rest of her life!

The children were greatly saddened to hear that Chrissie had gone to her eternal home. They could not remember home without Chrissie. Glen, who was still living in Vancouver, said he was not going to come to Toronto to her funeral. He wanted to remember Chrissie as she was when he last saw her. Several days after her death, Daisy received a letter from him,

Dear Mother,

Chrissie has moved up to higher service. Her service has been a life-long one to our family. To me, as long as I can remember, Chrissie has been an integral part of our home and life. She rejoiced in our successes and encouraged us through the difficult places. She constantly upheld each member of our family before the throne of Grace. The knowledge of this daily prayerful support was a source of comfort and strength.

This January day, we have lost a devoted friend, one of our own, but we would not wish her return from the presence of her Savior whom she has loved and served so faithfully for this useful span of years.

You, whose lives with Chrissie in these latter years have been so intimately interwoven, will miss her keenly. The Lord, who knows the end from the beginning, will sustain and support, and fill in the emptiness. There is a purpose, and He has a plan. It is only our duty to follow a step at a time—day by day.

Many lives have been touched by this little Irish lady and have been started on the way to Life Eternal, because she has passed this way.

And so I say—Good-bye, Chrissie,—we loved you dearly.

Glen

This letter summed up exactly how all the children felt about her. They were as devoted to her as she was to them and to their children.

Chrissie had three dreams in life, all of which came true before she died. She prayed constantly that Paul would go into the ministry and that God would make him not just a famous preacher, but that He would also make him a spiritual one. Her second dream was that she would some day make a trip to Vancouver where Glen was practicing as a gynecologist. This dream also was realized and she was so proud of Glen when she saw his Christ-centered home and family. Her third dream was that some day she would have the opportunity of crossing the sea to visit her homeland, Ireland. Daisy and Oswald made this desire a reality as well.

It was hard for Daisy to understand why God would take her from them now that they were getting older, but He always knows best and the day she was buried, they thanked Him for the forty-one years of her service, her friendship, and the spiritual blessing she had been to them. What the future held for them, they did not know, but as it has so often been said, at least they were assured of the One who holds the future.

After Chrissie's death in January, Daisy accompanied Oswald to Florida and all across the United States; while he held missionary conventions, she spoke to mass meetings of women. They introduced the faith promise offering to many churches that had never raised money for foreign missions before. It was a welcome chance to escape the cold, bleak Toronto winter, now that they were getting a little older. When they left, the sky was low and dark gray, a fine pelting snow was biting against the window pane, driven by a bitterly cold, blustery wind. Daisy felt that if she had stayed home the chill of the coming winter would settle down deep in her heart. The warm sunshine of Florida soon melted her spirit and heart and it was a joy to minister in a warmer climate. She never objected to the long winter months of snow when the children were home. They enjoyed the snow and ice; they could skate and sleigh ride. Those days were gone forever, and the love she once shared for winter with the children had gone. Winter had lost its excitement with the coming of the first snowfall. The children were gone—Chrissie was gone—life was different now.

Just as everything comes to an end, Daisy knew the severe cold of winter would end, followed by the glorious coming of spring when she would return to her family in Toronto.

"I don't think I would want to live where one season goes into another with little change in temperature or vegetation," she once said. "Nothing can equal the newness of joy and life that accompanies spring." They had left Toronto beneath the gray skies of winter, but now springtime was born in all its beauty. The song birds had come back; the sweet scent and loveliness of spring flowers filled the air. The great passion of the earth was evident on every side. Joy was restored and faith revived by the beauty of the change of season. April with new fresh life had been born from boisterous March. It was a time of resurrection, and Daisy was happy to be home again.

She was especially happy to be home in April, for this was the month of the annual missionary convention, and this time Paul, as pastor, was in charge of it. Paul would be making changes in the convention and Daisy was anxious to see how the people would respond. This would be the first time in forty years that her husband had not planned the convention in the church he had founded. His way had to come to an end and now everyone was looking forward to the new ideas of their new pastor.

Oswald had always continued the convention for four weeks and five Sundays, whereas Paul held it for two weeks. Oswald had used the Founder's Hall for the various missionary societies to set up their little booths laden with curios from the fields in which they were working. Times had changed, and since people had access to television programs and traveled more extensively, they were not quite as interested in seeing the curios. To replace these exhibits, he showed up-to-date pictures of the mission fields as the people were gathering for the services.

He still put up the great missionary mottos on the walls of the church, and took up the faith promise offering just as his father had done. Oswald used to read out every amount as it came in; the excitement mounted higher and higher the nearer they got to the goal set for the year. Instead, Paul announced the totals at various intervals throughout the service. So great was the giving, it would have been impossible to read out every amount.

Paul flew in Christian leaders from all over the world to challenge the people, because the new idea of training natives to spread the gospel in their own countries was now a much more effective way to speed up the evangelization of the world. Not enough natives were being trained when Oswald conducted conventions, so he had to rely upon the heads of different missions to relate what was being accomplished abroad by the missionaries. Paul felt it was important now to have a body of Christians in each country to carry on the work since no one knew how long missionaries would be admitted and allowed to work in different parts of the world.

Paul also introduced the idea of bringing in at least two hundred missionaries to attend the convention in order that they might learn what others were doing. The people of the church entertained them for the duration of the convention.

One inspiring evangelist came from the jungles of Africa. He became so excited when the total of the offering was announced that he literally jumped with joy to the pulpit. He said, in a voice loud and clear, and full of enthusiasm, his black face radiant, "You people have been carrying the load for all these years, sending missionaries to my continent of Africa, and if you think I have given you a vision, I want you to know that you have given me a new vision. I am going back to the jungle and I am going to conduct a faith promise offering amongst my people. I am going to teach them to trust God to prosper them enough so that they can give to missions. We are going to lift the load from you and carry it on our own shoulders." It was not long before The Peoples Church heard of the great results of his missionary convention deep in the jungle of Africa. How wonderful it was to think that the church in Canada could reach to the jungles of Africa with the burning flame of missionary zeal, and inspire Christians to have their own convention in that distant land.

The first year Paul was in charge, he was able to take on thirty-nine new missionaries and the offering amounted to much more than the goal he had set. Just as his father had done, he had a huge "thermometer" erected at the front of the church to record the totals as the money came in.

The building was filled with enthusiasm and excitement as the choir sang the "Hallelujah Chorus" after the grand total for missions was announced. Daisy was thrilled and thankful to God for His faithfulness as she witnessed Paul being used as his father had been to raise huge sums for missions. The promise God had given her years ago, "that he which hath begun a good work in you will perform it until the day of Jesus Christ" (Philippians 1:6), became increasingly real to her.

At the end of the summer, the equally beautiful golden days of autumn began, but this autumn was a special one for Daisy. It was September 12, 1966. Fifty glorious years had sped swiftly by since she had made that momentous decision to give up her freedom as a deaconess, to bind herself to home and husband. God's plan for her life had given her a greater freedom and opportunity to serve Him than she could ever have imagined. She looked back over the years when she first fell in love with the young preacher who had come to Dale Church, and who, much against her wishes, had usurped her position. She did not know then that her first love for him was just a taste of a flame that would grow brighter with the passing years.

As Daisy gazed out the window that September day, in the autumn of her life, she thought of the leaves of spring, how they stay bound to the branches of the trees, but then in the autumn, they become more beautiful, richer in color, full-blown, free to flutter to and fro, to romp and play, no longer bound, but free, free, gloriously free!

For Daisy and Oswald this was a golden day. They had not reached it by idle dreaming, but by enduring the refiner's tests of lives fully consecrated to God. They had found in their walk with God imperishable gifts of gold, worth more than anything else in life.

Their three children and nine grandchildren lovingly prepared a reception for them in their own home. Many of their friends called to share with them the way in which God had cared for them and blessed their ministry for fifty years together at home and abroad. At the reception Hope read a poem she had written for this occasion:

Fifty Golden Years

For fifty golden years they've trod
Together, hand in hand with God;

What blessings to the world they've brought
    As daily at God's throne they've sought
To serve Him with undying love
    Bestowed on them from Heav'n above.

As parents they have been pure gold,
    A heritage of worth untold;
In them their children look and see
    The gold that makes true honesty;
A gold that shines from deep within
    That all mankind would strive to win.

They've lived to show their flock the way
    To perfect peace and endless Day;
With faith unfaltering they've led
    Them thru the unknown path ahead;
They've guided them with hearts of love
    Inspired by God Himself above.

Across the seas to other lands
    They've carried out their Lord's commands;
A golden harvest crowns the years
    That they have lived thru joys and tears;
A great reward forevermore
    Awaits them on the Golden Shore.

Oswald and Daisy were touched by the sentiments expressed in this poem and they treasured it for years to come. It was the signature to a happy golden day representing fifty years of blessed wedded life.

The elders of the church surprised them the Sunday after their anniversary by presenting Oswald with a gold-plated clock-barometer-thermometer, and they gave Daisy an exquisite gold brooch as a token of their love for her. Letters and congratulations from all over the world were collected in a book they deeply treasured.

In the front of the book the elders had written: "As you gave your love to each other fifty years ago, we give to you our love tonight. Your prayers and sacrifices gave birth to The Peoples Church, a church now known throughout the world for its missionary endeavors."

Mayor Philip Givens of Toronto wrote: "Over the decades, the people of Toronto were privileged to turn to the familiar old landmark at the corner of Bloor and Park Road and gain comfort and strength by attending the inspirational meetings for which The Peoples Church is internationally famous."

Billy Graham, the most well-known evangelist of our time wrote: "You are an inspiration to us all. No two people in this generation have meant so much to the church in so many ways."

Gratitude and great joy welled up in Daisy's heart as she stood by her husband's side and was presented with fifty golden roses by the elders. But more meaningful than anything else that happened that Sunday evening was to see eighteen young people walk down the aisle to accept Christ as personal Savior at the close of Paul's message.

Daisy was now seventy-five years of age and was beginning to wonder if the Lord had any more work for her to do for Him and for others. She still loved to speak at meetings to women all over the United States and Canada but felt her overseas trips had come to an end, when Oswald, as excited as ever, overflowing with his everlasting zeal to visit mission work in other countries, announced that he wanted her to accompany him on yet another trip. This time it was to Scotland, Norway, Sweden, Finland, and Denmark.

Daisy felt she should go as long as she had a measure of good health and as long as she could help him in his undying service for God. She found traveling continually more strenuous as she grew older, but thanked God for giving her more than the promised threescore years and ten in which to serve Him.

It was a fascinating experience flying over Finland with its sixty thousand lakes spread out beneath them as far as they could see. It seemed to Daisy like eternal day in that country as it was still bright enough to read at 11:00 p.m. The sun rose at 2:30 a.m. In order to sleep blankets had to be draped over the windows at night.

After conducting thrilling meetings in Helsinki, presenting their missionary vision, they moved on to Stockholm with its beautiful lakes, inlets and waterways—truly an enchanting city. Daisy spoke many times to the women of Sweden, not fully realizing this would probably be her last trip overseas. She had already made nine world tours.

As she left these beautiful countries where one enjoys long hours of daylight, she found that the objects immediately surrounding her were slowly becoming enshrouded in darkness. After an eye examination the doctor said that it would be necessary to have cataracts removed. She had driven her car until she was eighty years of age, and now this and other activities had to be severely curtailed. She became more dependent on others. This was hard on one of her independent nature and disposition.

She decided she would like to be near her son Glen during her operation and recovery and so flew to Vancouver where the surgery was performed. Glen's wife, Kay, did everything possible to make her comfortable and happy in their home and Daisy was grateful to God for her loving care and for an opportunity to visit with her Vancouver grandchildren, June, Bruce and Christopher.

Shortly after she returned to Toronto, still hampered by poor eyesight, she suffered many falls, one resulting in a broken hip which caused her to be partially bedridden. However, she continued to be a great inspiration to her children and grandchildren and the many friends that came to visit her. June and Pauline were both nurses and loved to minister to her and listen to her many stories of her life and travels. During her two-week holiday June showed her deep devotion and love for her "Dais" by flying in from Vancouver to nurse her. Realizing that she might not have much longer to draw from her grandmother's wealth of experiences, June wanted to learn all she could from her.

One day as June was brushing her grandmother's soft silver hair, she observed, "Dais, all my friends these days are looking for freedom, and independence, but they seem to be searching in vain. Nothing satisfies them and gives them the liberty they seek."

As June lovingly massaged her neck and shoulders to relax her, Daisy replied quickly and in strong, deliberate tones, "The Bible says in John 8:32, 'Ye shall know the truth, and the truth shall make you free.' But what does it say in the preceding verse, verse 31? 'If ye continue in my word, then are ye my disciples indeed.' We have a choice to make. Discipline and obedience are the price of freedom, June, and together they bear the fruit of love. We must obey God's will, not ignore it. Because He loved us, Jesus obeyed the will of God, His Father, by sacrificing Himself on the cross for our sins to make us free. We must choose by what chains we will be bound in order to know freedom." Inspired by her thought-provoking words from Scripture, June lowered Daisy's head down on her pillow to rest. Then in a weaker voice hardly audible, she looked up at her granddaughter, and said, "This is what I have spent my life doing, telling women here and in faraway lands of this freedom, and now all I can do is silently pray that at least some of the seeds scattered will have fallen on good ground. I know that all those who have accepted this truth I will meet again at Jesus' feet."

14

Towards the Sunset

The brilliant shades of autumn were fast fading as the passing splendor of fall felt the icy winds of an early winter embracing her prematurely. As the evening shadows lengthened, the inevitable foreboding clouds were slowly gathering about Daisy as she lay motionless in her bedroom, too weak to move. Oswald, rising from his comfortable chair, obviously disturbed and restless, walked towards the window. As though transfixed, he gazed out upon what seemed to be the most dramatic sky he had ever seen. The heavens were fast filling with an ominous blackness amidst the lightning and sound of thunder rumbling in the distance. Beyond this darkness were deepening warm colors sweeping across a broad expanse of cloud formations in ever changing moods. As he looked on intently, his heavy heart was temporarily lightened by the silver lining highlighting the darkest cloud hovering over the fiery ball of the sinking sun in the west. Pondering the inevitable eventide of life, he thought that that storm cloud edged with silver symbolized a chariot that would some day convey Daisy victoriously to a brighter horizon.

As the sun set that unforgettable evening in the last part of October 1972, he felt as though an eternal night was wrapping its dreaded cloak about him. He knew unmistakably that the sands of time in Daisy's life were fast running out. Seated beside her bed, he tenderly clasped her feeble, bony hands in his. With sorrow piercing his heart and with a distant yet penetrating look of grief in his soft, blue eyes, he said, leaning a little closer to her, "Daisy, when you leave me, the sun will forever set in my life." Overcome by this deep sentiment of undying love so warmly expressed, she could only respond with eyes that glistened with tears of devotion. Uncontrollably they flowed down her cheeks, now wrinkled with the cares of this life. Although Daisy's spirit at times appeared to vacate her feeble frame as if beckoned to a fairer land, she bravely struggled to live, motivated by her intense desire to remain with her loved ones. Her will power continued strong and indomitable. For what repeatedly appeared to her family to be the end of the road was only another bend in the road, with more to follow in the ensuing months before she reached the final stage of her journey.

Another dreary day of painful lingering dawned, but this day was unlike all others for her and the family who kept a constant loving vigil. Glen, her elder son, felt constrained to fly to Toronto and spend what he feared would be his last treasured days on earth with his mother. She loved to hear him play her favorite hymns on the piano. "Glen," she said affectionately, "take me into the living room and play 'Jesus, lover of my soul, let me to thy bosom fly." Gently, he assisted her from her bed to the living room. Daisy, cautiously feeling her way, leaned heavily on his arm and sat close beside him. These precious moments, however, were brief, as he knew it was time to see her comfortably resting once more in bed. She had scarcely settled down, the inspiration of Glen's playing still lingering with her, when suddenly she edged herself forward into an upright position. With a strong voice, hardly expected of one so weak, she dramatically quoted the words of one of her favorite hymns, "The Unveiled Christ." "There He stands the mighty conqueror since He rent the veil in two," she said, repeating the words several times with great emphasis.

Seemingly her spirit had soared on the wings of faith into the Great Beyond—unknown, yet known to her and her God, for beyond this fine veil of death she caught a vision glorious of her Savior. As she neared the valley of the shadow it was apparent that she was relating to the death of Christ nineteen hundred years ago, of whom it is said in the Scriptures, "At noon darkness had fallen across the whole land for three hours, the light from the sun was gone and suddenly the thick veil hanging in the Temple, secluding the Holiest Place, was split apart from top to bottom, then Jesus cried, 'Father, I commit my spirit to you' and with those words, He died" (Living Bible—Luke 23:44-46).

Daisy knew the truth of the message which she had proclaimed for many years wherever she had traveled. Christ rose again, the mighty conqueror over that final enemy of death, making it possible for all who trust in Him as their Savior and High Priest to have direct access into His holy and eternal presence. She took courage knowing without doubt that the "certain hope of being saved is a strong and trustworthy anchor for our souls, connecting us with God Himself behind the sacred curtains of heaven, where Christ has gone ahead . . ." (Living Bible—Hebrews 6:19, 20). For Daisy, the doors of heaven stood ajar. Death was not the end, for in dying she would be born to eternal life. The last petal of this beautiful, fragrant flower was soon to fall to earth, but her spirit was to bloom forever in the garden of her new and permanent home.

It was a cold, crisp Sunday afternoon, when Peter, the eldest of her nine grandchildren, came to see her as he so frequently had done in the past. His visits with her were always a special occasion for he found himself the sole audience being highly entertained by Daisy's inimitable way of telling stories, which was not without a great deal of wit and drama. With her warm, understanding heart, she had the unique ability of bridging a gap of more than fifty years. She possessed a natural art of making the youngest generation perfectly relaxed and at home with her. Yes, it was always a special delight to visit with "Dais," as her grandchildren fondly called her. She was brighter and stronger that day, almost as if she were staging yet another comeback—a temporary recovery at least. Peter, however, unaware of this, had determined not to allow her to exhaust her limited reservoir of vitality and so had slipped through the front door of her home, expecting to find her in bed. But to his amazement, she was propped up in her favorite chair in the living room.

As he went to greet her, she affectionately cupped his face in her warm little hands and urged him to stay awhile and have tea with her. Though she usually loved to indulge in a little idle chatter at least, she was today in a deep, pensive mood. She lost no time in sharing with him her intimate thoughts. "Peter," she said, "I'll not be here much longer and there is something I want to tell you because you, like me, love all the finer things this material world can offer. But as I stand on the threshold of eternity, and look around at all I have and possess, I realize more and more, they are only things, Peter, only things! They seem so necessary but how unimportant they really are." Leaning forward, as if to whisper a secret, she continued, "When we bid farewell to this world we leave it all behind. We cannot take any of it with us. Only what we are in Christ and have done for Him will be of any worth and permanent value. Earthly pleasure and material gain are temporal but spiritual priorities are eternal. Never forget that, Peter."

Peter could scarcely comment. He had listened to this voice of experience since his childhood days. He knew she not only spoke with authority, having lived everything she believed, but somehow more disturbing to him was the realization that he was having his final intimate chat with her. Thoughtfully, after a few moments of contemplative silence, he responded briefly, "I'll not forget those words, Dais." Suddenly she reclined with a heavy sigh of weakness and weariness. Peter, momentarily alarmed, stood up. Then taking her by the arm he said, "I think it is time for you to have a rest, Dais." Somewhat preoccupied and saddened, he looked at his watch and added, "And I must prepare to leave for the airport." He had to return to his home in Vancouver. After making her comfortable in bed he reluctantly kissed her good-bye, knowing he had spent his last visit with her.

It was the final Sunday of the annual missionary convention in the spring of 1972. Oswald left for the service that evening with mixed emotions. He had high expectations of yet another victorious response in the giving to missions, but was deeply saddened by the fact that for the first time in forty-three years his beloved wife and strongest supporter in missions was unable to go with him. She was not left alone, however, for the friend she had met years before in South Africa, Norma Cooper, felt constrained to stay with her that night, knowing only too well the vacant longing that would be in Daisy's heart to attend. She had also promised Hope, who was overseas, that she would try to fill her place in her absence. Although Daisy had missed the services in the church for several months because of ailing health, yet somehow, not to be present that special night was as if a part of her had already died! As Norma sat with her in the living room, there was an obvious silence at 7:00 p.m., both knowing the final convention service had begun.

To Daisy's astonishment, Norma, looking across the room at her snuggled in her night apparel on the chesterfield, said, "Do you know what I would like to do for you tonight more than anything else in this world?"

Daisy, not quite sure what was in her mind, looked at her with curiosity and replied, "No. What?"

"I would like to bundle you up and take you to the church for the last twenty minutes of that great service so you can hear the grand total announced and the choir sing the 'Hallelujah Chorus.'" The sheer thought of such an unexpected possibility might have been what brought on a severe nose bleed! Swiftly, Norma took her to the bedroom to nurse her, despairing of any hope of making Daisy's dream a reality.

Seconds later, Norma was the one to be given the

surprised announcement for Daisy, lying flat on her back, looked up and said, "What will I wear?"

Elated by the sheer determination of Daisy's dauntless spirit, Norma ran to the telephone in the kitchen and dialed the church number. Excitedly she explained to the head usher, "Daisy Smith will be arriving at 8:15 p.m. Please prepare a comfortable chair for her." Knowing the auditorium would be packed to capacity, Norma made another request, "And please have two ushers ready to meet us when we get there, for Mrs. Smith is extremely weak."

They were hardly seated in the back row when, unknown to them, Paul had spotted his beloved, frail mother. Knowing the results of the final offering, Paul could scarcely contain his twofold joy! His face was radiant as he stepped forward to his pulpit. The audience was tense with silent anticipation. "The moment you have waited for has come," he said. "But I have two special announcements to make tonight. First, my mother, who has given her whole life to spreading the gospel through her missionary vision, and whom you've not seen now for many months because of ill health, is here tonight. This is her forty-fourth convention!" Spontaneously more than three thousand people rose to their feet and warmly applauded her. Daisy bowed her head and wept. Paul waited for the ovation to subside before he continued, "As the mother of missions in this church she is once more able to share in the rewarding results of our faith promise offering."

Oswald's face was aglow as quickly and excitedly his eyes scanned the crowd, trying to focus proudly on her. A silent hush fell momentarily on everyone as Paul paused to wipe his eyes. "And now, would everyone stand again, please, as I announce the grand total. You have given in these two weeks, $532,207.17. As a result of this offering The Peoples Church will once again be able to move forward in the sphere of world missions. We will add new workers to the four hundred already supported by this church." On this note, the choir sang jubilantly the "Hallelujah Chorus." Daisy, remaining seated, too weak to stand, could scarcely contain the joy and gratitude that welled up within her.

Her mind flooded with memories as the choir sang this glorious anthem. Her life seemed to flash before her. She saw herself as a young girl in Bible college studying diligently to equip herself to preach the gospel. She relived the days in the West Virginia mountains, struggling against untold odds to bring Christ's message of hope to those mountain people. She saw herself as a deaconess helping countless numbers in her own city of Toronto to find peace with God. She recalled the great conflict in her heart in making that far-reaching decision, whether to bind herself to home and husband or continue as a deaconess in the Dale Presbyterian Church, a work which had seemed so all-important then. Lost in the sanctuary of a myriad of sacred thoughts, she was startled when suddenly Norma touched her hand and said, "Mrs. Smith, the ushers are waiting to escort you to the car before the benediction is pronounced. We must avoid this great crowd. Many will want to talk to you but you are not strong enough." Quietly they slipped away.

Oswald lost no time rushing home. Bursting through the front door he hurriedly entered the bedroom. His face was beaming, yet he was noticeably shaken, still trying to recover from the shock of her stout effort to be present that night. Pacing up and down, his eyes dancing with glee he said, "To think, over half a million dollars was given for missions!" Then standing at the foot of Daisy's bed with an expression of amazement he looked down at her and added, "And you were there, a part of that great service. I never dreamed you could do such a thing. You really are a living wonder, Daisy."

Daisy could not resist dipping back into the past once more as she lay in bed exhausted from unduly taxing her limited strength. "I went on a journey into the past tonight, Oswald. As I looked over that vast auditorium of three thousand people, saw you on the platform with our son Paul in the pulpit, having just raised once again all that money to send the gospel to the ends of the earth. I could not help but think, What if I had not listened to God's voice so long ago? What if I had decided to remain a deaconess trying to compete, instead of complementing your ministry by joining forces with you in marriage? What if I had refused to be *bound to be free!*"

When people are about to leave their "old home" they eagerly focus their attention on their heavenly home. Stuart Hamblin's song, "This Ole House," was a favorite song of Daisy's and she delighted in the recording she had of it. As she was now, more than ever before, looking beyond and ever upward, she would ask her daughter Hope, who spent much of her time with her, to play the record for her. Thinking of her ever waning strength, yet never losing her sense of humor, she chuckled bravely and said, "Hope, I can just see this 'ole house' of mine falling to pieces and it wouldn't take much of a wind to blow it to the ground." Throwing her head back with a contagious laughter, she began quoting a verse of the song:

> Ain't gonna need this house no longer
> Ain't gonna need this house no more
> Ain't got time to fix the shingles
> Ain't got time to fix the door
> Ain't got time to oil the hinges
> Nor to mend the window pane
> Ain't gonna need this house no longer
> I'm gettin ready to meet the saints.

Shifting her position with added effort, she paused once more and then added contemplatively, "Yes, I am getting ready to move. This old house has lost its shingles. I no longer have the vitality I once enjoyed. Is it not strange, Hope, that the Bible says so much about life after death and yet at the same time is so vague about it?" Hope, deeply pained at the very thought of having to part with her beloved mother one day, sooner than she cared to think of, listened intently to every word of inspiration that fell from her lips. She knew in the years to come she would treasure every gem of truth spoken. Her only comfort would be memories of the words she spoke—many of them humorous, many profound.

Daisy, recalling the death of her brother, continued, "You know, Hope, Uncle Cress had a glimpse of heaven when he neared the end of his journey. He exclaimed, "It is unbelievably beautiful!" Turning her head and looking out the window she sighed, "Why is it that even though we know this is true, we tenaciously cling to this life?"

Hope, looking searchingly into her mother's eyes, said gently, "Mother, you have always taught me that to invest in this greater life we must be prepared to relinquish everything on earth for which we have striven." Then swallowing hard to fight back the tears, she continued, "But to leave the ones we love is a struggle and a more painful sacrifice."

Daisy, reaching out a feeble tiny hand to touch her daughter's face, whispered slowly, "I want to take you with me, but you will come some day. I am so old and so many of my friends have already moved on to their new life." Continuing to express her thoughts aloud she said, "How futile this life seems! Men struggle so hard to reach the top, making their investments in a shifting, shrinking world, as if this earthly life will continue forever. But I am getting ready to move, Hope," she once more reiterated emphatically.

Hope, raising her voice in reassuring tones, interjected, "Mother, Jesus so often spoke about leaving this earth and going to the Father. We who belong to Him will also be with Him one day. We are all journeying towards the sunset of this life and for those who know Christ it means spending eternity with our Creator. It is true, Mother, our vision of that mystic life hereafter is still blurred, but some things are so clear. We know it is our eternal home. It is a haven of peace without turmoil, joy without tears, rest without fear. We are only pilgrims in this life, not settlers," she continued. "This world is not our permanent dwelling place. The day will come for me, too, when I will have to take down my tent like a pilgrim and leave this earth to join you in our permanent home."

These precious moments were temporarily interrupted when the doorbell rang. It was Paul, who could scarcely bring himself to make his frequent visits to the home anymore. He knew each one could be the last.

245

Squaring his shoulders, as if bracing himself to bravely face whatever condition he would find her in, he quietly entered the bedroom. Daisy, having grown noticeably weaker since his last visit, trembling, reached out her hand to take his. Paul looked down on her wasting frame, her furrowed brow and sunken cheeks and tenderly kissed her. As he lingered beside her and stroked her silver hair, she said, "Paul, I'll not be here much longer. A mysterious veil lies between us and my eyes are growing dim, but I can see the glory surrounding our dear ones who are now with Him." Her voice then broke into a sob. This was especially disturbing to Oswald, yet he knew the tears she shed were soon to turn into everlasting pearls of praise to her Savior.

This was a dark hour, and yet a triumphant one for the family. They realized that the invisible mist surrounding Daisy was giving way to the first bright rays of heaven's glory. For her it was a soothing stillness, gently leading her into a life full of hope. Her spirit was slowly soaring upward along the unknown pathway, guided by the light of her Bright and Morning Star, Christ Himself, the King of Kings. Paul, overcome with deep love and profound gratitude to God for such a godly mother, stood speechless for a transient moment of apprehensive silence.

Oswald, sensing her departure was at hand, drew closer to her bedside and bowed his head in silent prayer. Don, Daisy's younger brother, who had taken his place as The Peoples Church pianist for over forty years, and his wife Bonnie, in loving support stood by Hope, who was seeking to console Ruth, Daisy's only living sister. Then Paul stepped forward, and holding both his mother's little

246